春 华 秋 实　饮 流 怀 源

献　给

小学老师

周淑芳

初中老师

吴兴华

高中老师

钟正欣

陈国声

黄炳文

曹静鸣

春华秋实·饮流怀源

我的计算机与金融研究

(1989—2004)

姚毓林　著

复旦大学出版社

作者简介

姚毓林，上海复旦大学计算机专业学士、美国纽约大学斯特恩商学院MBA、美国哥伦比亚大学计算机专业博士生。现为碧云资本执行合伙人，同时任纽约大学斯特恩商学院董事会成员和上海大学董事会成员。曾任美国路博迈亚太区副董事长兼董事总经理、美国艾威资本集团董事总经理、华安基金管理有限公司副总经理和首席投资官、美国贝伦斯资本合伙人等。曾任中国人民银行上海总部金融市场专家组成员、中国证监会QDII专家组成员。主要工作领域为投资管理、资产配置、风险管理。

1981年10月，与同学一同赴闵行探望小学班主任周淑芳老师（右三）；左一为笔者

1982年元旦，与同学一同探望初中班主任吴兴华老师（前中）；左一为笔者

1989 年 10 月，北京香山饭店，参加北京国际系统仿真及科学计算学术
会议，这是笔者第一次投寄国际会议论文

1990 年 5 月，上海工业大学，《一种新的知识表达方法研究》鉴定会；
站立者为笔者

1990年5月，上海工业大学，《一种新的知识表达方法研究》鉴定会；图左为方明伦教授

1990年，上海工业大学计算机视觉实验室；前排左一为洪进，后排左一为笔者

1990年9月10日，赴美前高中理科班老师来我家送行；自右向左分别为物理老师陈国声、数学老师黄炳文、笔者和化学老师曹静鸣

1990年9月17日，上海虹桥国际机场，家人送行，图右为陈英；这是笔者第二次坐飞机、第一次坐国际航班，美联航航班经停东京到旧金山入关，后转达美航班至亚特兰大

1991 年 8 月 24 日，亚特兰大，赴纽约当天一大早朋友们来送行；陈英在照片的背面写有详细文字，兹抄录如下："这是我们从亚特兰大出发时那天拍摄的，后面那辆黄色的大车伴着我们走了 2 000 公里，还是相当地气派吧！背景里的房子是毓林生活了将近一年的住房。（569 10th Street, Atlanta）"；右二为鲁明之，右三为笔者，右四为陈英，左一为相处近一年的室友（北京大学数学系毕业）

1998年5月9日，纽约大学MBA毕业；陈英贡献大，穿正式毕业礼服，真正的毕业生只能作陪衬

2005 年 9 月 25 日，相辉堂前大草坪，与家人访问复旦大学；后排为父亲，前排自右向左分别为岱菁、岱伟和笔者

2017 年 9 月，上海；离开贝伦斯资本回国后，始终与罗德尼·贝伦斯先生经常联系，2020 年前他几乎每年访问中国

2019 年 5 月 17 日，上海；罗德尼·贝伦斯先生（左一）访问我家，与我母亲（中）合照，右为笔者

2019 年 11 月 30 日，与马丁·格鲁伯教授（右）于纽约大学斯特恩商学院

2021 年 12 月 28 日，与陈国声老师（左）于第二届陈国声物理奖学金颁奖仪式

2022 年 9 月 9 日，与方明伦教授（右）于上海大学第 38 届教师节暨碧云资本校长奖颁奖仪式

2022 年 10 月 8 日，两位纽约大学斯特恩商学院 MBA 学生（父子俩）
与他们的教授暨商学院院长：中为拉古·森达拉姆教授（时任商学院院长），
右为岱伟（当时是 MBA 二年级学生），左为笔者

2024 年 6 月，与复旦大学前计算机系主任吴立德教授（右）合影

序一

———— 罗德尼·贝伦斯（Rodney Berens）

认识法兰克①是在 2001 年。我在 2000 年 11 月成立了一家公司贝伦斯资本（Berens Capital），目的是为投资者提供比他们自己创建的多/空股票对冲基金组合更好的投资组合。当时，大多数对冲基金投资者都是通过数据筛选出过往业绩最好的基金，并在几乎没有其他数据支持的情况下将资金在过往业绩最好的基金之间进行分配。而我们相信，过去的业绩并不能驱动未来的表现，人、流程和文化是业绩的驱动力。当时我们也认为，我们在"人"和"文化"方面的知识和经验已经足够。但我们很快就发现，自己缺乏量化能力，这不利于我们在评估"流程"方面为客户增加价值。我们需要引入量化能力，再加上更好的数据和系统支持，来帮助我们更好地理解基金经理的决策过程。

幸运的是，我们找到了法兰克。他接受了这份工作，并以惊人的精力、毅力和能力完成了任务。法兰克加入公司几个月后，我们意识到这个项目对于一家小公司来说非常艰巨，于是鼓励他找人帮忙。他找到了老朋友周侃，于是我们又引入了一位不知疲倦的团队成员。他们不眠不休地工作，终于创造出一套非常有用且在当时业内处于领先地位的工具。他们惊人的长时间工作离不开大量绿茶的支持。

为了了解这个项目的部分成果，您可以在本文集中找到 2004 年

---

① 本书作者的英文名字为 Frank（法兰克）。

发表在《财富管理杂志》(*Journal of Wealth Management*)上的一篇文章,题为"多/空股票对冲基金投资:行业专才基金比通才基金更好吗?"。法兰克撰写了这篇文章,布莱恩·克利福德(Brian Clifford)功不可没,而我的功劳较小。

法兰克于 2004 年 4 月离开贝伦斯资本回到中国,但我们的友谊一直保持至今。多年来,我们一直是好朋友。对流程的坚持和强大的量化分析能力仍然是帮助他成长的重要因素,这一点在这本文集与碧云资本的创立和成长中都有体现,碧云资本也拥有优秀的人才和非常强大的企业文化。他一直认为,在贝伦斯资本的经历以及随后我们之间的多次讨论,对他克服困难、思考如何建立自己的企业很有帮助,这让我受宠若惊。

我还了解他的家庭。他的家庭一直是他最大的热情和回馈所在。法兰克的智识有目共睹。他的工作能力非同一般,而且凡事都严于律己,遵守职业道德。而不那么显而易见的是,这些特质都沉淀在他始终开朗、乐观和善良的性格中。对于这一点,我始终无法理解,直到法兰克介绍我和他的父亲在上海见面——这是一位经历了许多磨难而仍然开朗、好奇、精力充沛的前辈。有其父必有其子。

文集中的许多其他文章对于像我这样非量化背景的人来说并不易读。不过,我还是强烈推荐《西蒙:活跃在科学前沿的博学家》一文,该文于 1989 年首次发表在《科学》杂志。我热衷于研究行为金融学,研究人类的情绪,如"恐惧与贪婪"之间的巨大波动以及其他偏见如何影响现实世界中的决策。这篇发表于 1989 年的关于西蒙的研究文章让我震惊,因为它在今天仍然具有可读性和现实意义。虽然我对人工智能和支持人工智能的算法知之甚少,但这篇文章详细介绍了人类对决策过程之理解的演变,以及人类是如何使用可以被客观描述和研究的具体决策过程的。如果你想进一步理解人工智能、算法或大数据,这篇文章将是有趣的资料性读物,非常值得花时间阅读。

继续努力向前，法兰克！也感谢你给我机会成为这本文集的一部分。

简 介

罗德尼·贝伦斯先生曾担任另类投资集团（Alternative Investment Group）的合伙人兼联席首席投资官。在加入另类投资集团之前，2000—2018 年他是贝伦斯资本管理有限公司（Berens Capital Management, LLC）的创始人兼联席首席投资官。1992—1998 年他在所罗门兄弟公司（Salomon Brothers）担任全球股票主管，且是公司全球运营委员会成员。在加入所罗门兄弟公司之前，他于 1975—1991 年在摩根士丹利（Morgan Stanley）担任董事总经理（Managing Director）、股票交易主管和全球研究主管。

他是摩根图书馆和博物馆（Morgan Library & Museum）的终身受托人和投资委员会主席，也在伍兹霍尔海洋研究所（Woods Hole Oceanographic Institute）担任投资委员会成员。他还是通用美国投资者公司（General American Investors）董事会和审计委员会成员。此前，他曾在斯隆基金会（Alfred P. Sloan Foundation）和彼得森国际经济研究所（The Peterson Institute for International Economics）的投资委员会任职。他还担任过极地黄金公司（Polyus Gold Mining Company）、基石物业（Keystone Property）、Storyfirst 通信公司（Storyfirst Communications）、美国证券交易所（American Stock Exchange）和全国投资专业人士组织（National Organization of Investment Professionals）的董事会成员。

他拥有宾夕法尼亚大学（University of Pennsylvania）学士学位和沃顿商学院（The Wharton School）工商管理硕士学位。

（主要由 DeepL 软件翻译，人工润色）

I first met Frank Yao in 2001. I had started a firm, Berens Capital, in November of 2000 to give investors a better portfolio of long/short equity hedge funds than they were likely to create for themselves. At the time most hedge fund selection was screening data for the highest performers and making allocations to the best performers with little additional data. We believed that people, process and culture drive performance and that past performance does not drive future performance. We believed our knowledge and experience on the "people" and "culture" side were sufficient. We quickly decided that our lack of quantitative skills was a handicap in adding value on the "process" side and that we needed them to help us better understand the manager decision-making process. We needed serious quantitative skills combined with better data and systems support. To our great good fortune, we found Frank Yao. He took the job and tackled it with amazing energy, stamina, and skill. Several months after Frank joined, we realized the enormity of the project for a small firm and encouraged him to find someone to help. He found an old friend Kan Zhou and we hired another tireless worker. They worked impossible hours and created in record a very useful and leading-edge tool for its time.

Their ridiculous hours of work were supported by the crazy amounts of Green Tea. To partially understand the output of this project you can find in this collection an article that appeared in *The Journal of Wealth Management* in 2004, titled "Long/Short Equity Hedge Fund Investing: Are Sector Specialists Better than Generalists?". Frank wrote this with deserved credit to Brian Clifford and less deserved credit to me.

Frank left Berens in April 2004 to return to China, and we have remained close friends over the intervening years. The belief in process and the strong quantitative skills remain an important part of his development and are on display both in this collection and at Green Court, a firm that also has great people and a very strong culture. I am flattered to think that his experience at Berens and the many subsequent discussions were helpful in overcoming and thinking how to build his own business. I have also gotten to know his family which have always been his greatest passion and reward. Frank's intellectual capacity is obvious to all. His capacity for work is extraordinary and he has a disciplined and ethical approach to everything. What is less obvious is that these traits are wrapped in an always cheerful, always optimistic and always kind personality. I could never quite figure this last piece out. That is until Frank introduced me to his dad. Here was this cheerful, inquisitive energetic man who had gone through a great deal of hardship. Like father, like son.

Many of the other articles in the collection are not easy for people like me who come from a non-quantitative background. That said, I would strongly recommend the article "Herbert Simon — An Active Learned Scholar in the Scientific Front," first published in *Science* in Chinese in 1989. I am an avid consumer of behavioral finance, of how human emotions like huge swings between "fear and greed" and other biases inform how decisions are made in the real world. This article done in 1989 on the work of Simon astounds me because it is so readable and relevant today. While I know very little about AI and the algorithms that support them, this article details the evolution of our understanding of decision making and how we came to the use of concrete processes that can be objectively described and studied. If you have gaps in figuring out AI, Algorithms, or Big Data, this article is a fun informative read and well worth the time.

Keep it up, Frank, and thank you for the opportunity to be a part of this collection.

Professional Biograph

Mr. Rodney Berens served as Partner and Co-Chief Investment Officer at Alternative Investment Group. Prior to joining Alternative Investment Group, he was the Founder and Co-CIO of Berens Capital Management, LLC from 2000 to 2018. From 1992 to 1998, he was Head of Global Equities and served on the Operating Committee at Salomon Brothers. Before Salomon Brothers, he was Managing Director, Head of Equity Trading and Head of Global Research at Morgan Stanley from 1975 to 1991.

He is a Life Trustee and Chair of the Investment Sub-Committee at The Morgan Library & Museum and a member of the Investment Committee of Woods Hole Oceanographic Institute. He is on the Board and Audit Committee at General American Investors. Previously, he served on the Investment Committees of the Alfred P. Sloan Foundation and The Peterson Institute for International Economics. He also served as a board member for Polyus Gold Mining Company, Keystone Property, Storyfirst Communications, the American Stock Exchange, and the National Organization of Investment Professionals.

He received a BA from the University of Pennsylvania and an MBA from the Wharton School.

序二

———— 方明伦

祝贺姚毓林先生的计算机与金融论文集出版!

姚毓林先生是我 20 世纪 80 年代的同事。他在复旦大学计算机专业本科毕业后,在上海工业大学机器人和机械自动化系暨上海机器人研究所从事教学和科研工作。他工作认真刻苦,非常努力,富有创新精神。他用世界银行的贷款购置设备,率先从事神经网络、模式识别、机器视觉方面的研究,短短 3 年多的时间,完成了多个科研项目,申请到国家青年基金,发表近 10 篇学术论文,主编一本供本科高年级学生使用的教材。虽然难说这样的成就在上海工业大学是唯一的,在当时他确实属优秀先进之列!

姚毓林先生有更高、更远大的目标追求。他于 1990 年 9 月途经日本、赴美国留学,首站在佐治亚理工学院(Georgia Institute of Technology)。这是一所国际著名的工科大学,有人工智能和机器人的研究方向,重视科教融合培养学生。学生除须参加必不可少的课堂理论教学,还必须完成项目。刚到美国,他的英语未完全过关,需要克服的困难多多,除了往家里打个电话报平安,其他时间都用于学习和研究工作,没有一点空闲时间,非常辛苦。当然收获也是丰硕的,为他以后的工作打下了扎实的、深厚的理论基础,培育了他独立从事科研工作的能力。其后,他获得纽约大学斯特恩商学院(Stern School of Business of New York University)工商管理硕士学位,并在哥伦比亚大学(Columbia University)读博士。需要强调的是,他获得了佐治亚理工学院和哥伦比亚大学的全额奖学金，选修了多门高等的数学课程，为他后来从事金融领域的工作驾轻就熟、卓有成效以及他的理性思考起了很有效的作用。

毕业后，姚毓林先生先后在美国道琼斯公司和高盛公司工作，曾任美国路博迈（Neuberger Berman）亚太区副董事长兼董事总经理等。现任碧云资本（Green Court Capital）管理合伙人。正因其有多方面的工作经历，积累了丰富、宝贵的经验，因此他得到了国内有关方面的重视。他曾任中国人民银行上海总部金融专家组成员。

姚毓林先生有一个难能可贵的好习惯：喜欢并善于在实践工作之后不断总结，进行理性思考，部分思考已写成学术性论文，发表在国际金融和工程专业杂志上。他有关投资方面的学术研究成果，已被英文投资专著和教材引用。如弗兰克·法博齐（Frank Fabozzi）和哈里·马科维茨（Harry Markowitz，诺贝尔经济学奖获得者）的近著 *The Theory and Practice of Investment Management*（John Wiley & Sons, 1st Ed in 2001, and 2nd Ed in 2011）。

姚毓林先生精选 10 篇在 1989—2004 年期间发表的论文汇编成册，主要集中于计算机和金融领域，这是件有意义的事情，对于在这两个领域从事实践工作、科研、教学和学习的广大读者都有参考价值。论文集只精选 10 篇，但内容较为宽广，涉及分布式计算机系统、Petri 网及应用、神经网络、模式识别、机器人视觉、知识表达、金融并行计算、股票价值估算、对冲基金的评估和选择等，尤其是关于西蒙（Herbert Simon）学术生涯评述一文，值得认真阅读。西蒙教授是人工智能的先驱、认知心理学家、诺贝尔经济学奖获得者，值得喜欢读人物传记的读者一阅，一定会有启迪。我还要特别推荐姚毓林先生写的后记，其中对每篇论文的来龙去脉、主要内容都有十分清晰的介绍。若先读后记，再读论文，效果可能会更好。

需要强调的是，姚毓林先生怀有感恩的拳拳之心。饮其流者怀其源,学其成时念吾师。他万分感谢他的父母、爱妻、儿女,同时对凡是对他有所帮助和支持的老师、同事、同学都表示深切的感谢,充分展示了我们中国人的情怀和美德。

我们国家正在进行中国式现代化建设,要实现伟大的民族复兴,建成金融强国,全面实现经济数字化,本文集的出版恰逢其时。计算机与金融领域的著作和论文很多,万紫千红,姚毓林先生的这本文集如一束精致的花朵。那就各美其美!

简·介

方明伦,上海大学终身教授,曾任上海大学党委书记兼常务副校长。清华大学本科毕业,英国曼彻斯特大学访问学者。曾任上海市智能制造(机械自动化)及机器人重点实验室主任、上海机器人研究所所长、国家教委(教育部)科技委委员、国务院学位委员会机械工程学科评议组成员、国家"863"计划 CIMS 主题下属的专题专家。主持研制"上海 2 号"和"上海 5 号"工业机器人,获上海市科技进步一等奖、国家人事部"国家级有突出贡献中青年专家"称号。编著教材和学术著作 8 部,发表学术论文 120 余篇。

序三

———— 马丁·格鲁伯（Martin Gruber）

在本书中，法兰克从他职业生涯里撰写的论文中精选了 10 篇他最喜欢的论文。法兰克的教育和工作经历横跨信息技术和金融管理领域，本文集反映了他广泛的兴趣和成就。我本人的专业领域是证券评估和投资组合管理，因此我的评论仅限于本文集中涉及这些主题的两篇文章。

第一篇文章《三项式红利估值模型》对金融学中最流行的证券估值模型之一进行了改进。1962 年的"戈登模型"（实际上由 J. B. 威廉姆斯于 1938 年首次提出）将股票的价值定为所有未来股息的现值，模型假定股票股息在所有时间段内每期都以恒定的速度增长。法兰克在他的论文中提出了一个估值模型，在这个模型中，每段时间的股息变化可以处于 3 种状态之一：以概率（P_U）增加指定的数额，以概率（P_D）减少指定的数额，或以概率（$1 - P_U - P_D$）保持不变。作者在模型中增加了一个额外的状态——破产，以及企业在任一时间破产的概率（P_B），从而使模型更加有趣。然后，他提出了在上述假设条件下估值问题的闭合解，并对 5 家公用事业公司的估值方案进行了检验。与"戈登模型"的早期形式相比，"姚模型"显示出更好的结果。

第二篇文章题为《多/空股票对冲基金投资：行业专才基金比通才基金更好吗？》，这篇文章分析了投资特定行业的对冲基金经理与投资多个行业的对冲基金经理的业绩对比。分析结果非常有趣，不在此赘述。我非常推荐这篇文章的方法论。作者认为,适当的基准应该是代表基金所投资的一个或多个行业的指数,回报、风险和风险调整回报必须根据适当的基准来衡量。这一见解纠正了商界和学术界最常见的错误之一。在认识到设计适当基准的重要性之后,作者利用最新的风险和收益模型来研究对冲基金的表现。每一位从业者在进行研究或解释他人的研究成果时,都应采用这篇文章概述的方法。

简　介

马丁·格鲁伯(Martin Gruber)是纽约大学斯特恩商学院的名誉教授和驻校学者,他曾在该学院担任金融学教授达 45 年之久。

他是美国国家经济研究局(National Bureau of Economic Research)投资委员会的董事和成员,是美国金融协会(American Finance Association)、金融管理协会(Financial Management Association)和金融量化研究协会(Institute for Quantitative Research in Finance)的会士(fellow)。他曾任美国金融协会主席,并在纽约大学担任金融系主任达 9 年之久。

他的著作《现代投资组合理论与投资分析》(*Modern Portfolio Theory and Investment Analysis*)(第九版)是美国商学院研究生院的主要教材之一。此外,他还出版了其他 6 本关于投资分析和投资组合管理的著作。格鲁伯教授撰写了 100 多篇文章,刊登在同行评审学术期刊上。

格鲁伯教授被美国东部金融协会(Eastern Finance Association)评为杰出学者,曾获得格雷厄姆和多德(Graham and Dodd)投资研究奖,并于 2004 年被AIMR 授予享有盛誉的詹姆斯·R. 维尔廷奖(James R. Vertin Award),以表彰他的研究对投资专业人员的长期指导意义。他曾担任 TIAA 董事会成员、CREF 董事会成员、CREF 董事会主席以及 S.G. Cowen 基金董事会成员。

格鲁伯教授拥有麻省理工学院(MIT)化学工程学士学位、哥伦比亚大学(Columbia University)生产管理工商管理硕士学位和金融与经济学博士学位。他还被比利时列日大学(University of Liege,Belgium)授予"名誉博士"学位。

更多信息请见 https://www.stern.nyu.edu/faculty/bio/martin-gruber。

(主要由 DeepL 软件翻译,人工润色)

In this volume Frank Yao has selected 10 of his favorite papers from those he has written over his career. Frank's education and work experiences span the fields of IT Modeling and Financial Management. His broad range of interests and accomplishments are reflected in this collection. My own expertise is in the field of Security Valuation and Portfolio Management and so I will limit my comments to the two articles in the volume dealing with these subjects.

The first article, A Trinomial Dividend Valuation Model, presents an improvement in one of the most popular security valuation models in Finance. The Gordon Model, 1962 (actually first proposed by J. B. Williams in 1938) values a share of stock as the present value of all future dividends. In the Gordon Model, stock dividends are assumed to grow at a constant rate each period for all time. In his paper, Frank Yao produced a valuation model where the dividend change over each period of time can be in one of three states: increase by a specified amount with probability (P_U), decrease by a specified amount with probability (P_D), or stay the same with probability ($1 - P_U - P_D$). The author makes the model even more interesting by adding an additional state: bankruptcy, with a firm entering bankruptcy at any time with probability (P_B). He then presents a closed form solution to the valuation problem under the assumptions described above and tests these solutions for valuing five public utilities. Comparisons with earlier forms of the Gordon Model showed that the Yao Model showed that it produced better results.

The second article, Long /Short Equity Hedge Fund Investing: Are Sector Specialists Better than Generalists, analyzes the performance of hedge funds managers who invest in specific sectors versus those who invest in multiple sectors. The results are interesting, but they are too numerous to reiterate here. I really recommend this article to you for its methodology. The author recognizes that the appropriate benchmark should be an index representing the sector or sectors in which a fund operates and that return, risk, and risk adjusted return must be measured against the appropriate benchmark. This insight corrects one of the most frequent errors in business and academia. Having recognized the importance of designing the appropriate benchmark, the author then uses the latest techniques of risk and return modeling to examine the performance of hedge funds. Every practitioner should employ the methodology outlined in this article whether doing research or interpreting the research results of others.

Professional Biograph

Martin Gruber is Professor Emeritus and Scholar in Residence at the Leonard N. Stern School of Business of New York University where he previously served as Professor of Finance for 45 years.

He is a director and a member of the investment committee of the National Bureau of Economic Research. He is a fellow of the American Finance Association, the Financial Management Association, and the Institute for Quantitative Research in Finance. He is past president of the American Finance Association and served as Finance Department Chairman at NYU for nine years.

The ninth edition of his book, *Modern Portfolio Theory and Investment Analysis*, is one of the leading texts in graduate schools of business. In addition, he has published six other books in investment analysis and portfolio management. Professor Gruber has written over 100 articles which have appeared in the peer-review journals.

Professor Gruber was named a distinguished scholar by the Eastern Finance Association, has received the Graham and Dodd Award for research in investments and in 2004 was awarded the prestigious James R. Vertin

Award by AIMR in recognition of his research notable for its relevance and enduring quality to investment professionals. He has served as a member of the board of trustees of TIAA, a member of the board of CREF, chairman of the board of CREF, and a member of the board of the S. G. Cowen Funds.

Professor Gruber holds an S. B. degree in Chemical Engineering from MIT and both an MBA in Production Management and a Ph. D. in Finance and Economics from Columbia University. He also was awarded the degree of Docteur "honoris causa" by the University of Liege, Belgium.

Full biography is available: https://www. stern. nyu. edu/faculty/bio/martin-gruber.

序四

—— 吴立德

.

很高兴看到姚毓林先生的论文集。

论文集由 20 世纪 80 年代到 21 世纪初这段时期中姚毓林先生有代表性的 10 篇论文组成，内容涉及计算机和金融两大领域。论文集的前 6 篇涉及计算机领域，后面 3 篇涉及金融领域，最后一篇是对活跃在科学前沿的博学家西蒙先生的学术生涯的评述。

计算机方面的 6 篇中有 4 篇都与 Petri 网有关，包括对 Petri 网的综述和应用 Petri 网对多种信息系统的建模与分析。特别在论文 "A Petri Net Model for Temporal Knowledge Representation and Reasoning"中，讨论了人工智能中重要的时间表示与推理问题，提出了一种基于时间 Petri 网的方法，它可以同时对时间点之间的定量关系和时间段之间的各种定性关系等进行表示和推理。论文发表在信息领域的著名期刊 *IEEE Trans. SMC* 上。这也实现了作者在复旦学习时对学术追求的一个梦想。

涉及计算机领域的其他两篇论文分别讨论用 Hopfield 网识别数字和计算多自由度摄像机参数的鲁棒区域。

涉及金融领域的有 3 篇。我对金融完全是门外汉，因此就不说了。好在，文集中的另外两篇序对此有很好的评述。

文集的序言和后记中包含了许多信息，从中可以看到作者在进行有关研究和写作时的工作与生活环境。

文集给我留下深刻印象的有两点。

　　一是作者对卓越的孜孜不倦的追求。不管是在大学学习期间，或是在教育科研单位工作期间，还是在金融行业工作期间，他都一直如此。这是十分难能可贵的！

　　二是作者一直怀有一颗感恩之心，因而一直有一个很好的"朋友圈"！

　　姚毓林先生已是一位十分成功的投资人。祝他事业蒸蒸日上！

简　介

　　吴立德，1958 年毕业于复旦大学数学系并留校工作。1975 年复旦大学成立计算机科学系时转入该系。1978 年越级晋升为副教授，1980—1981 年于美国普林斯顿大学和布朗大学做访问学者研究，1984 年经国家教委特批晋升为教授，曾任复旦大学首席教授。1982—1985 年任复旦大学计算机科学系主任，1995—2007 年任计算机科学与技术博士后流动站站长。

　　吴立德教授长期从事概率统计、计算机应用与软件方面的教学与研究。有著作 10 余种和论文 200 余篇，其中在国外期刊和国际会议上发表的有 70 余篇。获省部级以上奖励 10 余项。例如，他负责的"石油勘探地震资料的数字处理"获 1978 年全国科学大会奖，负责的"关于形状分析的研究"获 1986 年国家教委科技进步一等奖和 1987 年国家自然科学四等奖，著作《计算机视觉》获 1995 年全国优秀科技图书二等奖，负责的"计算机应用基础课程教学研究与实践"获 2001 年上海市优秀教学成果一等奖和国家优秀教学成果二等奖，负责的"语义视频信息检索的关键技术及其应用系统"获 2004 年上海市科技进步一等奖，等等。1988 年，他获批成为国家级有突出贡献中青年专家。

　　吴立德教授曾任国家自然科学基金会自动化学科评审组第二、第三、第四届成员(1988—1993)，国家自然科学基金会计算机学科评审组第六、第七届成员(1996—1999)，国家教委科技委员会计算机学科组第一、第二届成员，中国数学会第五届理事，中国计算机学会人工智能与模式识别专业委员会副主任，美国纽约科学院院士。

自序

　　2023 年年初,范景中先生赠送给我一本他的文集,由他的学生编辑整理,在序中他讲到"学者怕文章结集"。范先生是我们极为敬佩的大师,我的理解是,他希望继续推进他喜爱和感兴趣的学术研究,而不是告一段落。

　　计算机信息科学是我的本科专业,也是我早期学术研究的领域。就我而言,计算机方面的学术生涯在 20 世纪 90 年代已经基本结束。之所以这么说,有两个原因:一是计算机学科的发展极为迅速,对任何一个离开此领域前沿几年的研究人员而言,重新恢复和保持学术的敏感度将困难重重,从这个角度来看,本书收集的大部分计算机相关论文,其学术价值只具有历史意义;二是 90 年代在纽约时,我从计算机专业转到了金融行业。

　　那么,为什么要把好多年前写的论文结集成书呢?首先,论文集是对那段学术生涯做一小结。其次,可能也是更重要的,整理过程及论文集本身为我提供了一个很好的机会:感谢这么多年来老师、同学、同事、朋友和家人对我的支持和帮助,所以,编集实际上是一个感恩的过程。最后,不少当年的老师已是耄耋之年,这也增加了这项工作的紧迫感。

　　在很大程度上,范先生提供了最初的推动力;否则,这项工作很有可能永远没有启动的契机。

　　我将近 8 年的计算机学术研究可以分成两个阶段,以 1990 年

9月出国为分界线。

出国前

20世纪80年代我在复旦大学求学期间，没有做什么研究，主要是学习和参加活动。诸多同学聪明勤奋，表现优秀，我只是一个学习成绩一般的学生。印象最深的是当时刚从美国回来的系主任吴立德教授。吴教授在普林斯顿大学任访问学者期间解决了直线链码的Freeman猜想，其成果在 *IEEE Transactions* 上发表了。80年代初大陆学者在那样的顶尖学术期刊发表论文的屈指可数，吴教授也可能是最早的一位。这在当时对我们不仅仅是触动，更是震撼。吴教授是一座高山，高山仰止。那时候，我就有个梦想，什么时候自己也能够在 *IEEE Transactions* 上发表论文。

当时复旦大学计算机系有不少著名的教授和学者。除了吴立德教授之外，还有在国内最早开展数据库研究的施伯乐教授、软件理论专家钱家骅教授、算法理论的开拓者之一朱洪教授等一批国内顶尖的学者。难能可贵的是，许多教授亲自为本科生开课。例如，吴立德教授给我们上的"复变函数"、朱洪教授的"算法设计及分析"、汪嘉冈教授的"概率论"、徐建华教授的"图像处理"等，均为一时之选！

我的第一份工作，是在当时的上海工业大学机器人和机械自动化系暨上海机器人研究所做老师。当时的校长是著名科学家和教育家钱伟长先生，他强调两个中心，即教师以教学和科研并重，对科研尤为重视。方明伦教授是创系主任和创所所长，主持了上海最早的工业机器人研究和开发，之后即被钱校长委以副校长重任，专注于学校的科研领导工作（徐匡迪教授时任常务副校长，主持日常工作）。那时学校的科研气氛很浓。我所在的计算机视觉室（当时称为"检测二室"）由世界银行支持，配置有先进的电荷耦合器件（CCD）摄像头及相应的图像处理硬件和软件。原室主任因家庭原因赴美，系主任方明伦教授要求我临时负责视觉室(我当时 27 岁),给了我极大的信任,也是巨大的动力和压力。方教授营造了宽松而高要求的学术环境,为我今后的科研工作和个人发展打下了坚实的基础。

本书选取的 5 篇论文(第一、第二、第三、第四和第十篇)是我在上海工业大学工作期间完成的。第一篇为一个分布式系统的通讯协议的形式描述和分析,是我正式发表的第一篇国内学术刊物论文。第二篇是对一个并发实时系统的形式描述和分析,是我发表的第一篇国际学术刊物论文。第三篇为 Petri 网的综述,有幸发表在国内著名的《自然》杂志上。第四篇实现了人工神经网络对数字模式的识别,发表于中国自动化学会会刊《机器人》杂志。第十篇对著名的人工智能先驱、认知心理学家和诺贝尔经济学奖获得者西蒙的学术生涯做了评述,发表于百年老刊《科学》杂志。在上海工业大学期间,我还承接了一个横向项目"计算机发型设计系统的设计和开发",即对人脸关键点进行识别,再与预存的发型库进行匹配。虽然人脸千差万别,但以当时的技术手段,我们已能对几乎所有人脸做相当好的识别。虽然没有发表论文,但这应该可以被看作早期人脸识别的一次有意义的探索。

出国后

1990 年 9 月,我来到美国,前 9 个月在佐治亚理工学院学习,这主要是一个语言、文化的适应阶段,几乎没有做什么研究。1991 年到哥伦比亚大学后,我围绕知识表达和机器人视觉开展了一些研究工作(第五和第六篇论文)。第五篇提出了一个有关时态知识表达和推理的模型,发表在 *IEEE Transactions on Systems, Man and Cybernetic* 上,终于实现了我在复旦大学读本科时的学术追求梦想。我们的研究条件比吴立德教授当时的条件要好不少,所以出成果相对容易。第六篇计算了机器人视觉场景中多约束下的鲁棒视点。

本书中有 3 篇论文(第七、第八和第九篇)是我到金融行业工作后所写。第七篇使用分布式并行计算系统来计算复杂的金融衍生品。第八篇是我在纽约大学斯特恩商学院读"part-time MBA"的时候，受马丁·格鲁伯教授和当时高盛的同事鼓励，发表在 *Journal of Portfolio Management* 上，此后还被收入哈里·马科维茨[1]和弗兰克·法博齐主编的教科书[2]。在贝伦斯资本工作期间，我写了不少研究札记，其中有一篇(第九篇)发表在《财富管理杂志》上。

这个时期发表的论文绝大部分是计算机领域的，少量与金融相关。出国前后，我总计有近 20 篇论文发表在学术期刊、杂志上和收于国际会议论文集中。有些文章的初稿参加国际会议，终稿在学术期刊上发表。

本书结构

本书选取了 9 篇论文提交终稿或修改稿，涉及的领域有分布式计算机系统、实时系统的形式分析、Petri 网及应用、神经网络、模式识别、机器人视觉、知识表达、金融并行计算、股票价值估算、对冲基金的评估和选择，再加一篇西蒙学术生涯评述文章，共计 10 篇。6 篇用英文发表，4 篇用中文发表；8 篇发表于学术期刊和杂志，2 篇收录于国际会议论文集。所有论文以原貌呈现，不做改动。每篇文章的后记集中附于书后，主要叙述当时为什么做这方面的研究、文章是怎么写的、解决了什么问题及相关的信息，后记也为我提供了感谢、感恩的机会。如果读者觉得这些论文太枯燥，可以直接跳到书后阅读后记。

斗换星移，春华秋实。我们这一代人，如果有些微不足道的成

---

[1] 现代组合理论(Modern Portfolio Theory，MPT)创始人，1990 年诺贝尔经济学奖得主。

[2] Frank Fabozzi and Harry Markowitz, *The Theory and Practice of Investment Management* (1st and 2nd Editions), John Wiley.

就,是因为赶上了改革开放的好时代,更是来自一路上许多人的鼓励和帮助。古人云:"落其实者思其树,饮其流者怀其源。"这正是本论文集成书之主要目的。

遗憾的是,限于篇幅,本书不能一一罗列所有应该感谢、感恩的人。求学生涯与回国之前工作的数十载只是人生的一个章节。

此为序。

2023 年 8 月 20 日初稿

2024 年 6 月 10 日端午节修改

目
CONTENTS
录

1

消息传输协议 MTP 的 Petri 网模型和分析 *

一、消息传输协议(MTP)

MTP (Message Transmission Protocol)是为一个分级分布式微机系统 HDMCS (Hierarchical Distributed Micro-Computer System)的通讯软件设计的消息传输协议,采用总线式结构。目前的系统由一台 IBM PC(或兼容机)和两台高级单板机 FD-SBC-51 组成,单板机采用 Intel 公司生产的 MCS-51 系列单片微计算机做处理机。

在 MTP 中,将要发送的一块数据分成多个消息帧,然后依次地发送。MTP 规定,在发送每个消息帧之后,接收计算机(目标结点)送回一个应答信息,以告知发送计算机(源结点)本次传输是否已正确接收。若经 CRC (Cyclic Redundancy Check)检验正确,说明已正确接收了这帧消息,则目标结点回送一个"确认"(ACK)信息;如果 CRC 检验出错,说明传输等有差错,目标结点就回送一个"否认"(NAK)信息。进一步从时间推进的角度考虑,在源结点发送下一帧消息之前,源结点要等待来自目标结点的应答信息。如果源结点收

* 定稿。发表于《微电子与计算机》(航天工业部一类工程技术月刊,中国计算机学会会刊)第 6 卷第 1 期,1989 年,第 1-6 页。

到 ACK，它就继续传输下一个消息帧；如果收到的是 NAK，它就重发该帧消息。重发这帧消息的次数有一确定的限值(可由用户设定)。如果同一消息帧重发次数已超过重发限值，那么，很可能在线路上或者在源结点或目标结点内部已存在故障。对于该故障状态，必须发信息给系统，以便系统做相应的处理。图 1 给出的是有差错重发的消息交换顺序。

为了防止出现图 2(a)(c)中所示的情形[即源结点发出的消息帧在传输途中丢失或目标结点做出的应答信息(ACK 或 NAK)受到干扰而丢失，不能正常地发送到目标结点或源结点，使得结点 A 将无限等待下去]，在系统中设置了超时限值，当发送方的等待应答时间超过了这一限值时就做超时处理，以避免系统瘫痪[参见图 2(a)(d)]。

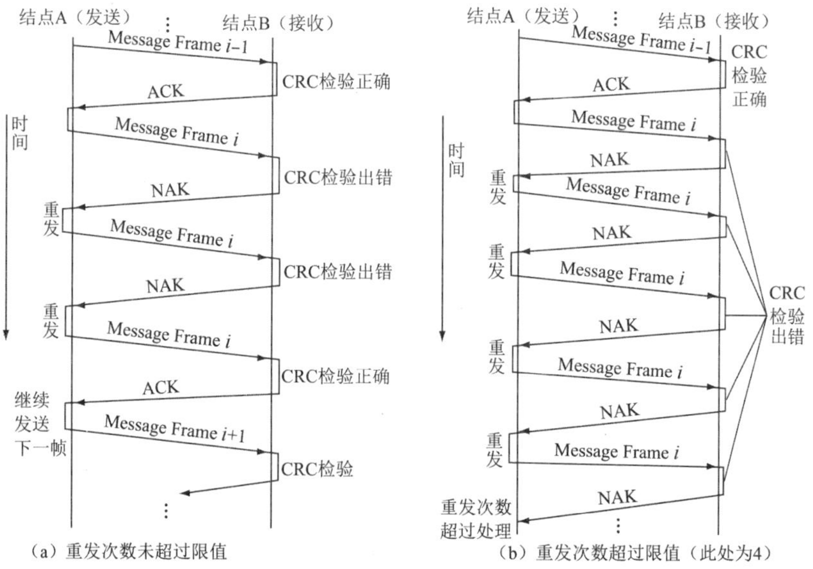

图 1 有差错重发的消息交换顺序

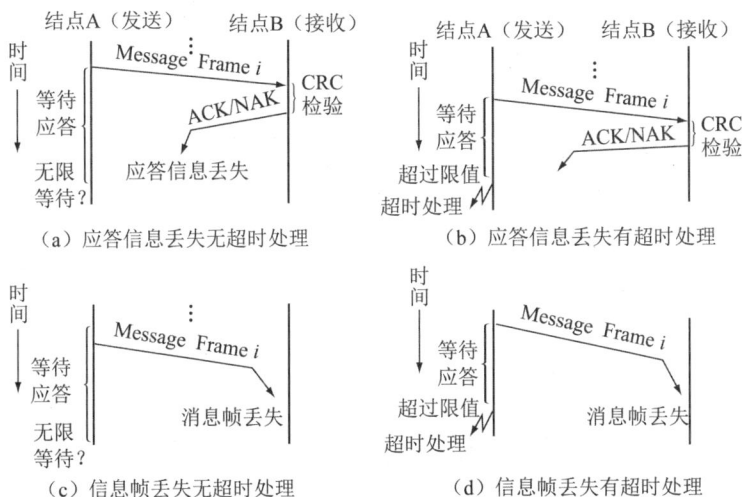

图 2　信息丢失超时处理的消息交换顺序

二、 Petri 网的有关概念和定义 [1, 2]

Petri 网是一有向图,具有两种结点:一种是"位置",一般用圆圈表示;一种是"转移",一般用直线段表示。Petri 网可用三元组 $N = (P, T, A)$ 表示,其中,$P = \{p_1, p_2, \cdots, p_n\}$,是位置的集合;$T = \{t_1, t_2, \cdots, t_m\}$,是转移的集合;$A \subseteq \{P \times T\} \bigcup \{T \times P\}$ 为结点间有向弧的集合,它定义两种函数 I 和 O:对每个转移 t,其输入位置集合为 $I(t) = \{p \mid (p, t) \in A\}$,输出位置集合为 $O(t) = \{p \mid (t, p) \in A\}$。如果用 t 表示事件,$I(t)$ 表示该事件发生的条件,$O(t)$ 就表示事件发生的结果。这样,Petri 网可用来表示系统的静态性质。

为了表示系统的动态性质,在位置中放入一些标志(Token),在图中用黑点表示。Petri 网的标记 M 是一映射:

$$M: P \to I,$$

其中，$I = \{0, 1, 2, \cdots\}$。M 把 Token 分配给网中的位置。一般地，可将 M 视为一个向量，其第 i 个元素 $(M)_i$ 表示分配给 p_i 的 Token 的数目，一个带有标记 M 的 Petri 网 $N = (P, T, A)$ 称为带标记的 Petri 网 $C = (P, T, A, M)$。

在一个带标记 M 的 Petri 网 $C = (P, T, A, M)$ 中，对转移 t，若 $\forall p \in I(t)$，均有 $M(p) > 0$，则称该转移 t 是可行的。对于可行的转移 t，将其每个输入位置中的 Token 消去一个，且在它的每个输出位置中增添一个 Token，则称此时该转移 t 实施或点燃（fire）了。实施的结果产生一个新的标记 M'，在这里

$$M'(P) = \begin{cases} M(p) + 1, & p \in \dot{O}(t), p \notin I(t), \\ M(p) - 1, & p \in I(t), p \notin O(t), \\ M(p), & \text{其他}。 \end{cases}$$

若一个 Petri 网到达了所有转移都不可以实施的标记，则称该网是死锁的（deadlock）。

在带标记的 Petri 网 $C = (P, T, A, M)$ 中，若转移 t 对于每个 $M' \in R(\dot{M})$［可达集合 $R(M)$ 是从 M 可达的所有标记的集合］都存在一从 M' 可达的标记，使 t 在这个标记中是可行的，则称转移 t 是活的（live）。在一带标记的 Petri 网中，若每个转移都是活的，则称该 Petri 网是活的。

三、消息传输协议 MTP 的 Petri 网模型

考虑传输介质为理想状况，即既不出差错也不丢失消息帧和应答信息的情况。图 3(a) 给出了在这种情形下相继发送/接收两帧消息的 Petri 网模型。

图 3(a) 中，在初始状态下，p_{11} 和 p_{21} 中各有一个标志，分别表示已准备好发送第 i 帧消息和已准备好接收第 i 帧消息，此时 t_{11} 是可行的，实施 t_{11} 表示源结点发送了一帧消息。t_{11} 实施后，将 p_{11} 中的标志移去，在 p_{01} 和 p_{12} 中各放入一个标志，p_{12} 表示等待应答，p_{01} 表示源结点发送了一帧消息，此时 t_{21} 是可行的，实施 t_{21} 表示目标结点接收了该帧消息。t_{21} 实施后，将 p_{01} 和 p_{21} 中的标志移去，在 p_{22} 中放入一个标志，并使得 t_{22} 可行，说明目标结点已正常接收该帧消息。t_{22} 实施后，将 p_2 中的标志移去，在 p_{02} 和 p_{23} 中各放入一个标志，分别表示回送一协议信息给源结点和该帧消息接收完毕。t_{12} 实施说明源结点已接收到目标结点的确认消息。实施 t_{13} 后，标志到达 p_{14}，同时 t_{23} 实施说明消息帧接收完毕，标志到达 p_{21}。此时，p_{14} 和 p_{24} 中各有一个标志，表示已准备好发送第 $i+1$ 帧消息和已准备好接收第 $i+1$ 帧消息，又可以继续传输。

下面考虑在非理想传输介质中的消息传输，即可能有差错需要重发，可能有信息丢失需要超时处理的情形（参见图 1 和图 2）。

文献[3-6]对信息丢失的情形建立了一些 Petri 网模型，但这些模型都是针对下述情形的，即发送方在超时时间限值内等不到接收方的应答信息 ACK，就重发帧消息。实际上这里隐含着两种可能：①发送的消息或应答信息 ACK 丢失；②可能是接收方"否认"接收的消息（如消息的 CRC 检验出错）。文献[3-6]中的模型仅讨论了前一种情况，因此，这些模型不适合本系统的消息传输协议。为了建立本系统的消息传输协议（MTP）的 Petri 网模型，在上述正常传输模型的基础上，增加了信息（发送的消息帧或 ACK 或 NAK）丢失和传输有差错发送方重发的情形，图 3(b) 给出了这种情形下相继发送/接收两帧消息的 Petri 网模型。图中模型没有对图 1 中的重发限值做限制。

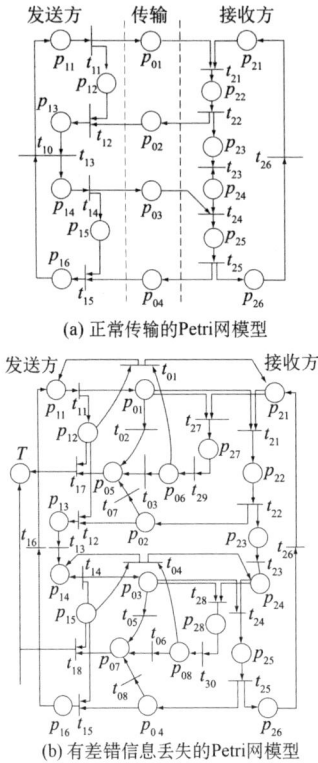

图中各位置和转移的含义

p_{01}，p_{03}：序号为i，$i+1$的消息帧在传输中

p_{02}，p_{04}：序号为i，$i+1$的"确认"在传输中

p_{05}，p_{07}：序号为i，$i+1$的信息（消息帧/ACK/NAK）的丢失

p_{06}，p_{08}：传输对序号i，$i+1$的消息帧的"否认"（NAK）

p_{11}，p_{14}：准备发送序号为i，$i+1$的消息帧

p_{12}，p_{15}：等待序号为i，$i+1$的应答；

p_{13}，p_{16}：序号为i，$i+1$的消息帧发送完毕

p_{21}，p_{24}：准备接受序号为i，$i+1$的消息帧

p_{22}，p_{25}：序号为i，$i+1$的消息帧被正常接受

p_{23}，p_{26}：接受序号为i，$i+1$的消息帧完毕

p_{27}，p_{28}：序号为i，$i+1$的消息帧接收异常（否认）

T：超时处理（如退出发送状态并告知系统等）

t_{01}，t_{04}：重发序号为i，$i+1$的消息帧

t_{02}，t_{05}：序号为i，$i+1$的消息在发送时丢失

t_{03}，t_{06}：对序号为i，$i+1$的消息帧的"否认"信息的丢失

t_{07}，t_{08}：对序号为i，$i+1$的消息帧的"确认"信息的丢失

t_{11}，t_{14}：发送序号为i，$i+1$的消息帧

t_{12}，t_{15}：接收序号为i，$i+1$的"确认"

t_{13}，t_{16}："产生"序号为$i+1$，$i+2$的消息帧

t_{17}，t_{18}：发送序号为i，$i+1$的消息帧时的等待应答超时

t_{21}，t_{24}：接收序号为i，$i+1$的消息帧

t_{22}，t_{25}：发送序号为i，$i+1$的"确认"

t_{23}，t_{26}：序号为i，$i+1$的消息帧接收完毕

t_{27}，t_{28}：发送对序号为i，$i+1$的消息帧的"否认"

t_{29}，t_{30}：传输序号为i，$i+1$的"否认"

(a) 正常传输的Petri网模型

(b) 有差错信息丢失的Petri网模型

图3　消息传输协议(MTP)的 Petri 网模型

四、 Petri 网模型的分析

以下利用标志机器（Token Machine）[6]的分析工具对图 3（b）给出的 Petri 网模型进行分析。

Petri 网可以到达的所有可能状态，以及它们之间可能的转移定义了一个标志机器。图 3（b）中初态 p_{11} 中有一个标志，p_{21} 中有一个标志，则只有转移 t_{11} 是可行的，在 t_{11} 实施后从 p_{11} 中移去标志，在 p_{12} 和 p_{01} 中各添入一个标志，这时 Petri 网到达状态 $p_{01} p_{12} p_{21}$。在该状态下，或者 t_{27} 实施，或者 t_{02} 实施，或者 t_{21} 实施，表示动作发

生的顺序是非本质的。继续上述过程，即可得到相应于图 3(b) 的 Petri 网模型的标志机器，如图 4 所示。相应于图 3(a) 的 Petri 网模型的标志机器较简单，故略去。

根据上述标志机器的定义及前两节所述的 MTP 内容和 Petri 网的概念，从图 4 的标志机器中可以看到图 3(b) 中的 Petri 网模型及其所描述的消息传输协议的性质：

(1) 一个消息帧发送后，接收方可以根据是否有差错，告知发送方应答信息（NAK 或 ACK）；

(2) 对信息（消息帧或者 NAK，ACK）的丢失，使用超时的方法告诉系统，以免瘫痪；

(3) 有差错时重发该帧消息；

(4) 该 Petri 网模型中无死锁现象；

(5) 该 Petri 网模型是活的。

在这里，(1) 至 (3) 是该 Petri 网描述的消息传输协议的性质，(4) 和 (5) 则是描述消息传输协议的 Petri 网模型的性质。图 3(b) 的 Petri 网模型没有对重发限值加以限制，因此在图 4 的标志机器中一旦收到"否认"（NAK），就重发该消息帧。在实际系统中重发限值由用户确定，因此不会发生永远重发下去的情形，图 4 中以虚线表示这一情况。因此，系统的消息传输协议的设计是合理的。

我们使用 Petri 网理论的工具对 MTP 建立了模型，并进行了分析，从而得出协议的设计是合理的结论。使用约 2 500 条汇编语言指令，在 HDMCS 中已顺利地实现了 MTP，并达到了预计的通讯协调目标，与理论分析的结论一致。

本文根据文献[7]改写。原文是在孙振飞副教授指导下写成的，并承蒙复旦大学施伯乐教授、上海交通大学陈铁年教授及上海计算所徐培南副研究员等审阅，在此一并表示感谢。

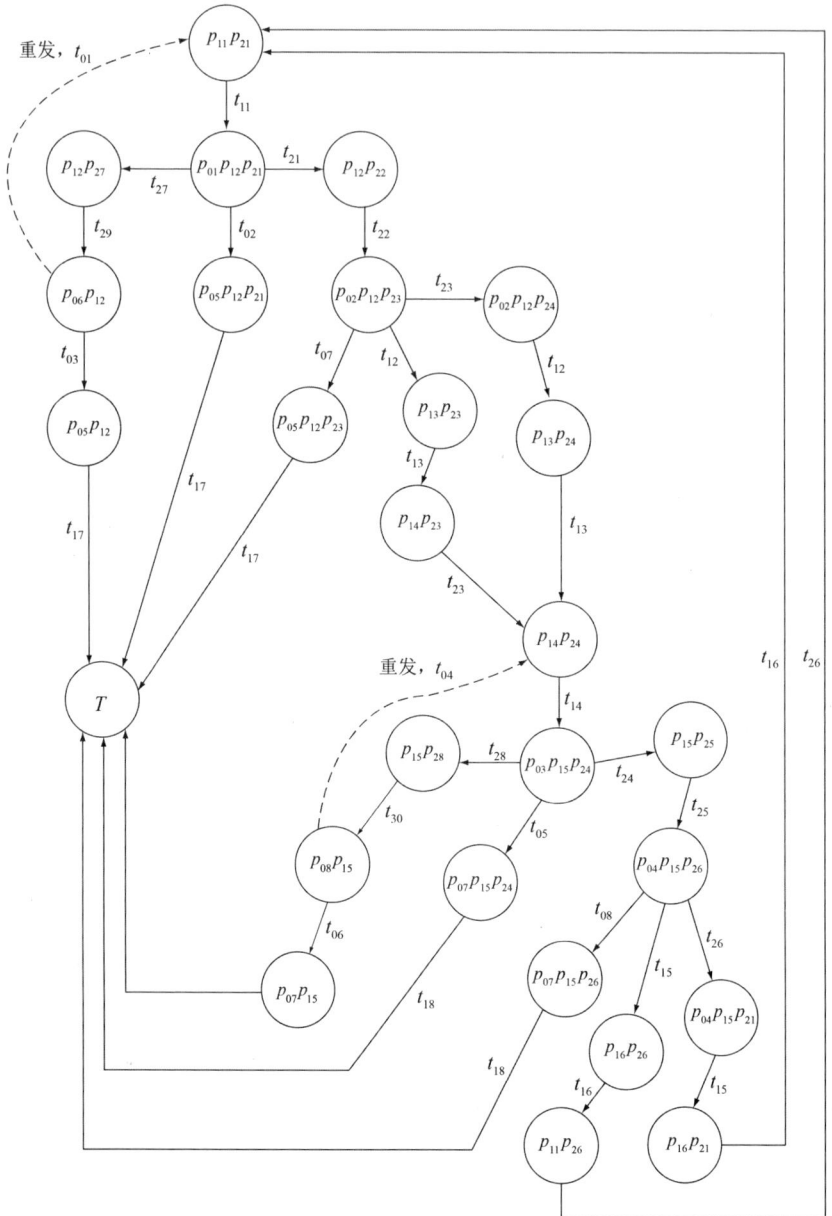

图 4　Petri 网模型的标志机器

参考文献 *

［1］ J. L. Peterson, "Petri Net", *ACM Computing Surveys* Vol. 9, No. 3, Sept. 1977, p. 223.

［2］ T. Agcrwala, "Putting Petri Net to Work", *Computer* Vol. 9, No. 12, Dec. 1979, pp. 85-94.

［3］ M. Diaz, "Modelling and Analysis of Communication and Cooperation Protocol Using Petri Net Based Models", *Compute Networks*, Vol. 6, No. 6, Dec. 1982, pp. 419-441.

［4］ M, K. Molloy, "Performance Analysis Using Stochastic Petri Nets", *IEEE Trans. on Computer* Vol. C-31, No. 9, Sept. 1982, pp. 913-917.

［5］ M. Diaz, "Petri Net Based Models for the Specification and Validation of Protocols", in *Advanced in Petri Nets* 1984, *Lecture Notes in Computer Science*, Vol. 188, Springer Verlag; New York, 1985, pp. 101-121.

［6］ P. M. Merlin, and D. J. Farber, "Recoverability of Communication Protocols Implications of a Theoretical Study", *IEEE Trans. Communications* Vol. COM24, Sept. 1976, pp. 1036-1043.

［7］ 姚毓林, "HDMCS——一个分级分布式微机系统", 上海工业大学, 1987 年.

---

* 出版说明：本书中选取论文的参考文献使用发表时的格式，并未作全书统一处理。

2

An Approach to Formal Specification and Analysis for Time Performance of the Concurrent Real Time System (RTEXS) [①]

1. Introduction

As real time systems become more widely used, interest has increased in techniques and tools which can be used to model and evaluate their performance. Petri net models have been recommended by many researchers as useful tools for modelling and evaluating distributed systems[1-3], communication protocols[4-6] and so on. The basic Petri net model[7, 8] is a general model of computation which can be used to model the control flow, concurrency, and synchronization in the system. This basic model can be analyzed to determine if the system being modeled contains deadlocks or undesirable states. The weakness of the basic model is its inability to model timing relationships between events. Over the past decade, the timed Petri net, which is established by introducing the notion of time into the Petri net model, has made it easier to analyze the performance

① Final draft. Published in *International Journal of Computers in Industry* (Elsevier Science Publishers B. V.), 1989, Vol. 12, pp. 347–354.

parameters of these systems. [9-13] Performance influences all aspects of computer systems, from their design to management. Hence, it is important to study in detail a system's performance parameters at every stage of design. It is especially important to be able to analyze and predict the performance of a newly designed system since actual performance measurement is intractable. [11]

This paper uses a timed Petri net to model a real time concurrent system RTEXS (Real Time EXecuting System) to analyze and yield useful performance estimates (the minimum time needed for one cycle of the system). This is very important to meet the real time requirements of a real time system. Section 2 gives an overview of the timed Petri net. Section 3 describes the procedure of the method of the performance analysis for the system using a timed Petri net and an overview of the RTEXS system which has been designed and implemented by the author. Section 4 provides the timed Petri net model of the system and illustrates in detail the method as used for the analysis of performance of the RTEXS system. Conclusions are given in Section 5.

2. Timed Petri Nets and Analysis Method

Timed Petri nets (TPNs) were first introduced by Ramchandani[9] by associating firing times to the transitions of ordinary Petri nets (PNs), in order to study their steady state behavior. Since then, many researchers have reported their works on TPNs. [9-13] In some cases, fixed times have been used, leading to deterministic models. In others, random firing times have been associated with transitions, resulting in stochastic TPN models. [14] Sifakis[10] has associated fixed delay times with the "places" of PNs and shown that, given a set of relations describing the behavior of such a TPN, its maximum computation rate can be found. Garg[11] uses this TPN to model and analyze the communication protocol. We have chosen Sifakis's TPN to model and analyze the RTEXS system in this paper.

Sifakis and Garg have defined and represented TPN as follows.

Definition. A timed Petri net (TPN) is a 6-tuple $N = (P, T, \alpha, \beta, \tau, v)$, where

P is a set of places $(P \neq \varnothing)$;

T is a set of transitions $(T \neq \varnothing,$ and $P \cap T = \varnothing)$;

$\alpha: P \times T \to \mathbf{N}$, is a forward incidence function (with $\mathbf{N} =$ the set of natural integers);

$\beta: P \times T \to \mathbf{N}$, is a backward incidence function; $\tau = (\tau_0, \tau_1, \cdots, \tau_i, \cdots)$ an increasing sequence of real numbers called time base; and

$v: P \times T \to \tau$ is a mapping such that for all $(p, \tau_i) \in P \times T$: $v(p, \tau_i) = \tau_j \to \tau_j \geqslant \tau_i$.

Representation. To a TPN one can associate a digraph whose nodes are the places and transitions represented by circles and bars, respectively. There is a directed edge from place p_s to transition t_j if

$$\alpha(p_s, t_j) = n_{s,j} \neq 0.$$

There is also a directed edge from transition t_r to place p_w if

$$\beta(p_w, t_r) = n_{w,r} \neq 0.$$

A marking M of a PN, shown by dots (called tokens or markers) in the place p, is a mapping of P into $\mathbf{N}$:

$$M: P \to N.$$

Rules

(a) A token in a TPN may be in one of the two following states: available or unavailable. Initially, each place p contains $M_0(p)$ available tokens.

(b) A transition t is enabled iff every place p_s which has a directed edge to t contains $\alpha(p_s, t)$ available tokens at least.

(c) The firing of a transition t has to take place instantaneously, as it is enabled. It consists in removing $\alpha(p_s, t)$ available tokens from each of the places p_s and in placing $\beta(p_w, t)$ tokens in each place p_w which has a directed edge from t. The transition firing "takes no time": if the firing of a transition is initiated at an instant τ then it is supposed to terminate at the same instant τ.

(d) A token remains unavailable in a place p_s during the time interval z_i, after which it becomes available.

Sifakis has studied the behavior of pure TPN's such that

$$\forall (p, \tau) \in P \times T \; v(p_i, \tau) - \dot{\tau} = z_i = \text{constant}.$$

i.e., each token is delayed by a time z_i in the place independently of its arrival.

For a TPN with n places and m transitions, the incidence matrix C is defined as

$$C = [c_{ij}]_{n \times m}$$

with

$$c_{ij} = \begin{cases} \beta\ (p_i,\ t_j), & \text{if} \neq 0, \\ -\ \alpha\ (p_i,\ t_j), & \text{if}\ \alpha\ (p_i,\ t_j) \neq 0, \\ 0, & \text{otherwise.} \end{cases}$$

Sifakis has studied the case where the firing frequencies of the transitions are constant, and the corresponding TPN has a periodic functioning and I is a solution of

$$CI = \mathbf{0},\ I > \mathbf{0}. \tag{1}$$

Each entry i_k of the current vector I represents the frequency of the firing transition t_k in the one cycle. The vector I depends on the initial marking and the delays associated with the places. Another relation that I must satisfy is

$$\{J'_s M\ (\tau_0) \geqslant J'_s \mathbf{Z} C^+ I\}_{s=1}^k, \tag{2}$$

where J is a place-invariant of the net, $(J_1,\ J_2,\ \cdots,\ J_k)$ is the set of place-invariants corresponding to the set of elementary subnets of the net, $(A'$ denotes the transpose of $A)$, $C^+ = (c_{ij})$ with

$$c_{ij} = \begin{cases} \beta\ (p_i,\ t_j), & \text{if} \neq 0, \\ 0, & \text{otherwise} \end{cases}$$

and Z is the delay square matrix given by Diag $(z_1,\ z_2,\ \cdots,\ z_n)$.

The relations (1) and (2) describe the steady-state behavior of the TPN. For every periodic functioning, the current vector I satisfies these relations but the converse is not always true: a solution I_0 of these equations does not necessarily correspond to a feasible periodic functioning from M_0. This is due to the fact that (2) takes into account only the imposed delays z_i. In fact, the delay of a token in place p_i is the sum of the delay z_i and of a variable "synchronization" delay due to the waiting of a token for other tokens to become available.

Let I_0 be a current vector of the TPN. Then I_0 is said to correspond to a functioning at a natural rate if I_0 satisfies the set of n linear equations given by

$$CI = 0, \ I > 0, \tag{1}$$

$$\{J'_s M (\tau_0) = J'_s ZC^+ I\}_{s=1}^{k} \tag{3}$$

where $\{J_s\}_{s=1}^{k}$ is a base of the space of solution of $C' X = 0$.

Functioning at natural rate corresponds to functioning at maximal rate: the delays of tokens in the places are exactly equal to their unavailability times z_i. Obviously, every solution of this system of equations is a maximal solution of (1) and (2). Consequently, for every vector I corresponding to a feasible functioning there exists a solution of (1) and (3) such that

$$I_0 \geqslant I.$$

In the following sections, we have interpreted this I as corresponding to the maximum (possible) computation rate of the net, with the given values of the delays z_i.

3. Procedure of Analysis, RTEXS System

3.1 Analysis Procedure

The procedure used to analyze the performance of systems modeled by means of a timed Petri net can be divided into five steps: [11]

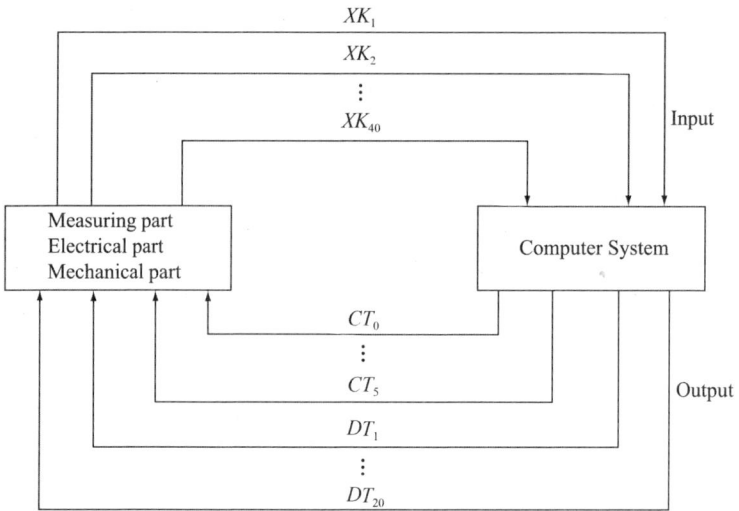

Fig. 1 Automatic miniature bearing assembling computer control system

(1) Build a detailed TPN diagram of the function of the system. Use "places" to represent its conditions, and "transitions" to represent its operations and events.

(2) Reduce the TPN as much as possible, by disregarding, for example, the places and transitions not concerned with performance issues.

(3) Analyze the TPN model of the system to obtain the various possible distinct transition sequences of operation of the system. This is done by solving the equation $CI = 0$, for the net, where C is its incidence matrix. Find also the independent solutions of the equation $J'C = 0$.

(4) Draw the relative subnets of the TPN, one for each I vector and J vector.

(5) For each sequence of transitions I, write down the time taken to complete the sequence by inspection from each J vector subnet.

if $3XK*4XK*5XK*8XK*9XK*10XK=1$
then $DT_2, DT_5=1, DT_{17}, DT_{18}, DT_{19}=0$;
Delay T_1; $DT=0$.

Legend:
XK_i ($i=1, 2, \cdots, 40$): input conditions;
DT_i ($i=1, 2, \cdots, 20$): output results;
CT_i ($i=0, 1, \cdots, 5$): output results;
T_i ($i=1, 2, \cdots, 12$): delay time.

if $1XK*6XK=1$ then $DT_{45}=1, DT_{16}=0$,
$CT=1$; Delay T_2; $CT_1=0$.

if $2XK*7XK=1$. then Delay T_3.

$DT_{13}, DT_{14}, DT_{15}=0$
Delay T_8; $CT_2=1$;
Delay T_9; $CT_2=0$.

Delay T_4; $DT_3=1, DT_4=0, CT_0=1$.

if $23XK*24XK*26XK*=1$
$DT_8=0, DT_9=0, DT_{10}=1, CT_5=1$;
Delay T_{10}; $CT_5=0$

Delay T_5; $CT_0=0$.

$DT_{20}=1$; if $15XK*19XK=1$ then $DT_{17}=1$;
if $16XK*18XK*(\backslash21XK)*(\backslash22XK)*34XK=0$
then $DT_{18}=1$;
if $17XK*18XK*(\backslash21XK)*(\backslash22XK)*34XK=0$
then $DT_{19}=1$.

if $20XK=1$ then $DT_6=0$;
Delay T_{11}; $DT_6=1$;
if $20XK*40XK=1$ then $DT_{12}=1$.

if $3XK*4XK*8XK*9XK=1$
then $DT_1=1, DT_2=0$.

if $5XK*10XK=1$
then $DT_1, DT_3=0$;
Delay $T_6, DT_5=1$;
Delay $T_7, DT_5=0$.

if $28XK=1$ then
DT_7, DT_{10},
$DT_{11}=0$

if $33XK=1$ then $DT_{11}=1$
if $(37XK=1)\vee(38XK=1)$
$\vee(39XK=1)$ then $DT_7=1$

if $11XK=1$ then $DT_{13}=1$.

if $19XK=1$ then $DT_{12}=0$;
if $12XK*19XK=1$ then
$DT=1, DT_9=0, DT_{14}=1$;
if $13XK*19XK=1$ then $DT_{15}=1$;
if $14XK*19XK=1$ then $DT_{16}=1$.

if $(\backslash37XK)*38XK$
$*27XK=1$
then $CT_3=1$.

if $37XK*(\backslash38XK)$
$*27XK=1$
then $CT_4=1$.

if $25XK=1$ then $DT_8=0, DT_9=1$.

Delay T_{13};
$CT_3=0, CT_4=0$.

if $29XK=1$ then $DT_{20}=0$.

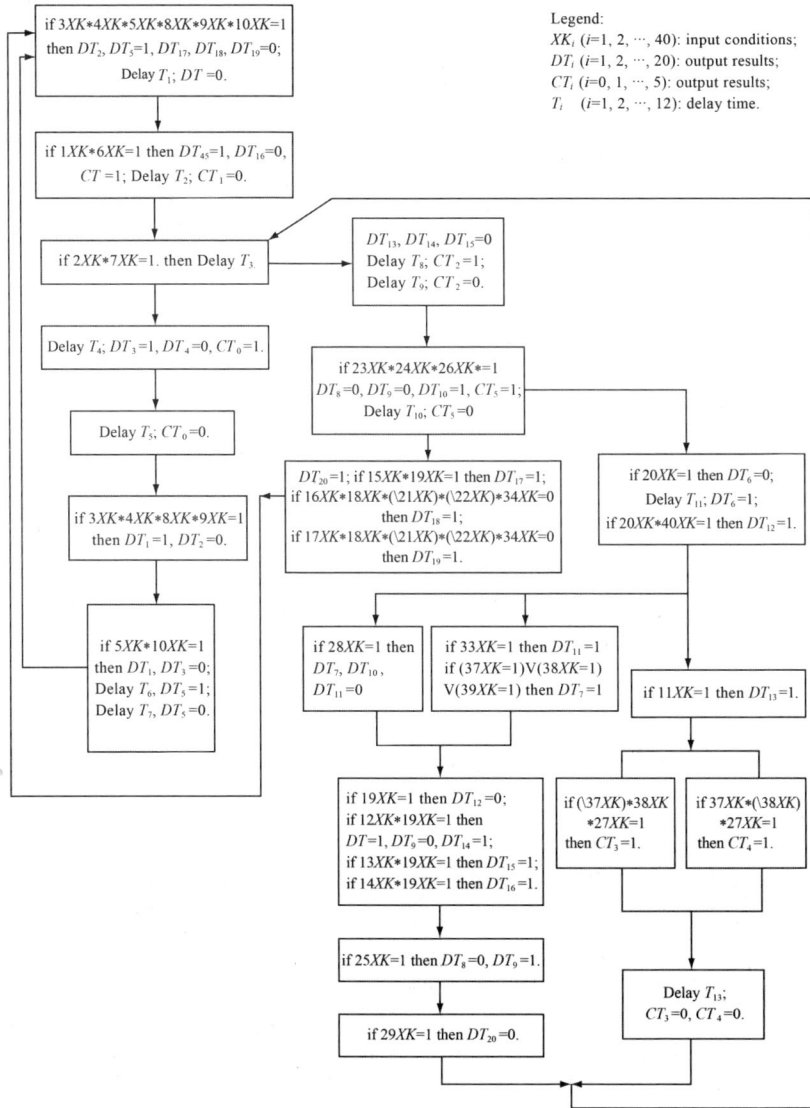

Fig. 2   The action flow of the automatic assembling machine

This can be done by adding the time delay z_i of the places p_i of the subnet for J which are involved in completing this sequence. The time taken for each sequence I is the largest of times given by the J subnets.

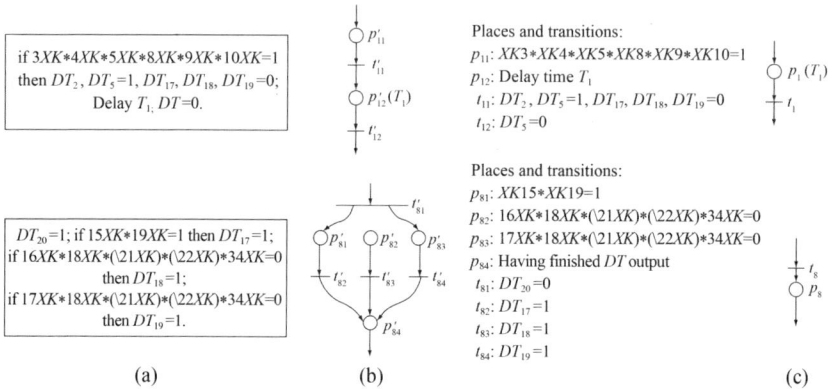

if $3XK*4XK*5XK*8XK*9XK*10XK=1$ then $DT_2, DT_5=1, DT_{17}, DT_{18}, DT_{19}=0;$ Delay $T_1, DT=0.$	p'_{11} t'_{11} $p'_{12}(T_1)$ t'_{12}	Places and transitions: p_{11}: $XK3*XK4*XK5*XK8*XK9*XK10=1$ p_{12}: Delay time T_1 t_{11}: $DT_2, DT_5=1, DT_{17}, DT_{18}, DT_{19}=0$ t_{12}: $DT_5=0$	$p_1(T_1)$ t_1
$DT_{20}=1$; if $15XK*19XK=1$ then $DT_{17}=1$; if $16XK*18XK*(\backslash21XK)*(\backslash22XK)*34XK=0$ then $DT_{18}=1$; if $17XK*18XK*(\backslash21XK)*(\backslash22XK)*34XK=0$ then $DT_{19}=1.$	t'_{81} p'_{81} p'_{82} p'_{83} t'_{82} t'_{83} t'_{84} p'_{84}	Places and transitions: p_{81}: $XK15*XK19=1$ p_{82}: $16XK*18XK*(\backslash21XK)*(\backslash22XK)*34XK=0$ p_{83}: $17XK*18XK*(\backslash21XK)*(\backslash22XK)*34XK=0$ p_{84}: Having finished DT output t_{81}: $DT_{20}=0$ t_{82}: $DT_{17}=1$ t_{83}: $DT_{18}=1$ t_{84}: $DT_{19}=1$	t_8 p_8
(a)	(b)		(c)

Fig. 3　The process of modelling and reducing for the system using timed Petri nets (TPN). (a) Action flow. (b) Corresponding TPN. (c) Reduced TPN model.

If there is only one possible J vector, then the time taken for each I sequence is equal to the time found from that J subnet.

3.2 The RTEXS System

The RTEXS system is a software system for controlling an automatic miniature bearing assembling machine (Fig. 1). The hardware part consists of the measuring-instrument, electrical and mechanical apparatus. There are forty inputs (XK_i, $i = 1, 2, \cdots, 40$), and twenty six outputs (CT_i, $i = 0, 1, \cdots, 5$; DT_i, $i = 1, 2, \cdots, 20$) for the computer system. The outputs of the computer system depend on input conditions and delay times. The detailed work process of the automatic assembling machine is not given in this paper. The action flow diagram of the RTEXS system for the control of the automatic miniature bearing assembling machine is given in Fig. 2. In this paper, it is supposed that the production of the input conditions is instantaneous and independent.

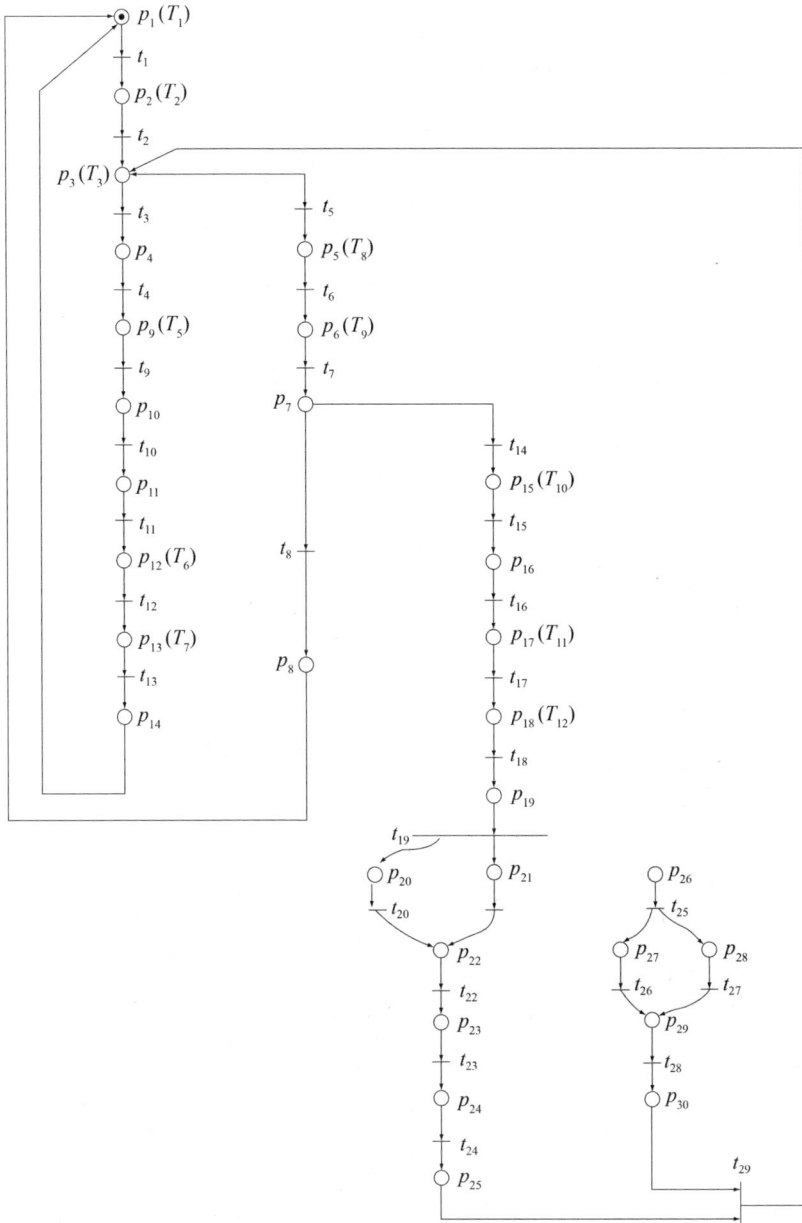

Fig. 4   The TPN model of Fig. 2

4. The TPN Model and Analysis of the RTEXS System

4.1 The TPN Model of the RTEXS System

Two examples are given to illustrate the process of modelling for the system given in Figs. 1 and 2, see Figs. 3(a) and (b). The result of reducing the detailed TPN model of Fig. 4 is also provided, see Fig. 3(c). The reductions do not affect the results of the TPN to model and analyze the system.[7] The detailed TPN model of the RTEXS system and reduced TPN model are given in Figs. 4 and 5, respectively. All labels of places, transitions and time delays are rearranged in Fig. 5, and

$$z_1 = T_1 + T_2,$$

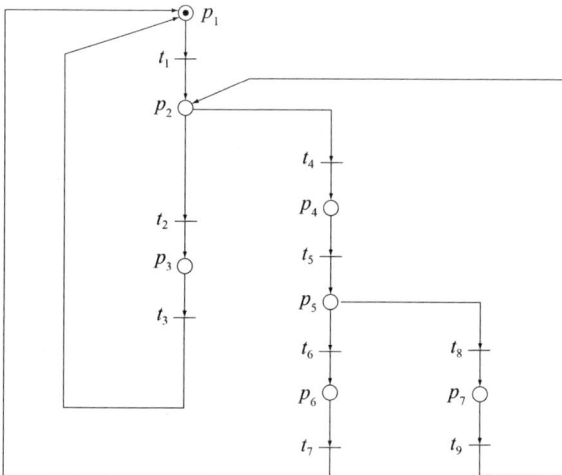

Fig. 5 Reduced TPN model of Fig. 4

$$z_2 = T_3,$$
$$z_3 = T_4 + T_5 + T_6 + T_7,$$

$$z_4 = T_8 + T_9,$$

$$z_5 = z_6 = 0,$$

$$z_7 = T_{10} + T_{11} + T_{12} + T_{13}.$$

4.2 Analysis of the TPN Model

We have, for Fig. 5,

$$\mathbf{Z} = (z_1,\ z_2,\ z_3,\ z_4,\ z_5,\ z_6,\ z_7),$$

$$\mathbf{M}'(\tau_0) = (1\quad 0\quad 0\quad 0\quad 0\quad 0\quad 0),$$

$$\mathbf{C} = \begin{vmatrix} -1 & 0 & 1 & 0 & 0 & 0 & 1 & 0 & 0 \\ 1 & -1 & 0 & -1 & 0 & 0 & 0 & 0 & 1 \\ 0 & 1 & -1 & 0 & 0 & 0 & 0 & 0 & 0 \\ 0 & 0 & 0 & 1 & -1 & 0 & 0 & 0 & 0 \\ 0 & 0 & 0 & 0 & 1 & -1 & 0 & -1 & 0 \\ 0 & 0 & 0 & 0 & 0 & 1 & -1 & 0 & 0 \\ 0 & 0 & 0 & 0 & 0 & 0 & 0 & 1 & -1 \end{vmatrix}.$$

$\mathbf{CI} = \mathbf{0}$ has three solutions given by

$$\mathbf{I}_1 = (1\quad 1\quad 1\quad 0\quad 0\quad 0\quad 0\quad 0\quad 0),$$

$$\mathbf{I}_2 = (1\quad 0\quad 0\quad 1\quad 1\quad 1\quad 1\quad 0\quad 0),$$

$$\mathbf{I}_3 = (0\quad 0\quad 0\quad 1\quad 1\quad 0\quad 0\quad 1\quad 1).$$

$\mathbf{J}'\mathbf{C} = \mathbf{0}$ has one solution given by

$$\mathbf{J}' = (1\quad 1\quad 1\quad 1\quad 1\quad 1\quad 1).$$

The various subsets representing these vectors are given in Figs. 6 (a)-(c), respectively. For each $\mathbf{I}$ vector, the maximum rate of computation can be written from the inequalities

$$\mathbf{J}'\mathbf{M}(\tau_0) \geqslant \mathbf{J}'\mathbf{ZC}^+\mathbf{I}.$$

Thus we have, for the sequence of transitions given by I_1,

$$i_{1max} = \min[\, 1/(z_1 + z_2 + z_3)\,]\,,$$

for the sequence given by I_2 we have

$$i_{2max} = \min[\, 1/(z_1 + z_2 + z_4 + z_5 + z_6)\,]\,,$$

and for the sequence given by I_3 we have

$$i_{3max} = \min[\, 1/(z_2 + z_4 + z_5 + z_7)\,]\,.$$

Conversely, we can state that the minimum times taken for one cycle of each sequence to be completed are

$$
\begin{aligned}
T_{min} &= \max[\,(z_1 + z_2 + z_3)\,] \\
&= z_1 + z_2 + z_3 \\
&= T_1 + T_2 + T_3 + T_4 + T_5 + T_6 + T_7,\ \text{for } I_1, \quad (4)
\end{aligned}
$$
$$
\begin{aligned}
T_{min} &= \max[\,(z_1 + z_2 + z_4 + z_5 + z_6)\,] \\
&= z_1 + z_2 + z_4 + z_5 + z_6 \\
&= T_1 + T_2 + T_3 + T_8 + T_9,\ \text{for } I_2, \quad (5)
\end{aligned}
$$
$$
\begin{aligned}
T_{min} &= \max[\,(z_2 + z_4 + z_5 + z_7)\,] \\
&= z_2 + z_4 + z_5 + z_7 \\
&= T_3 + T_8 + T_9 + T_{10} + T_{11} + T_{12} + T_{13},\ \text{for } I_3. \quad (6)
\end{aligned}
$$

The permissible range of time delays $T_i\,(i = 1, 2, \cdots, 13)$ in the RTEXS system is as follows,

$$T_1 = 5 - 8,\ T_2 = 2 - 4,$$
$$T_3 = 1 - 3,\ T_4 = 4,$$
$$T_5 = 10,\ T_6 = 7 - 9,$$
$$T_7 = 5 - 8,\ T_8 = 7 - 9,$$
$$T_9 = 2 - 4,\ T_{10} = 2 - 4,$$
$$T_{11} = 5 - 8,\ T_{12} = 5 - 8,$$
$$T_{13} = 2 - 4.$$

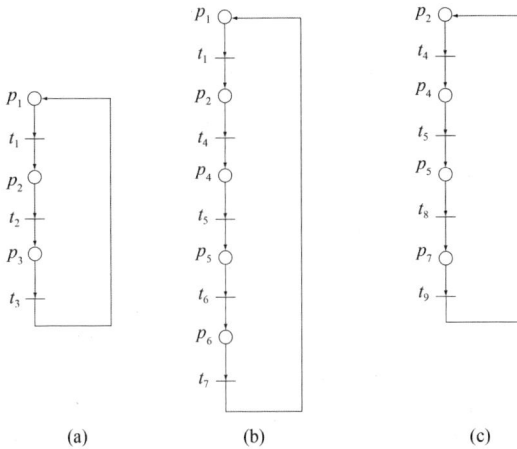

Fig. 6   (a) Subset for I_1. (b) Subset for I_2. (c) Subset for I_3

If the upper limit value for each time delay is chosen, i. e., $T_1 = 8$, $T_2 = 4$, etc., then we can state that the minimum times taken for the completion of one cycle of each sequence under the worst case of the system are

$$T_{min} = 46 \text{ for } I_1,$$
$$T_{min} = 28 \text{ for } I_2,$$
$$T_{min} = 40 \text{ for } I_3.$$

If the lower limit value for each time delay is chosen, i. e., $T_1 = 5$, $T_2 = 2$, etc., then the minimum times taken for completion of one cycle of each sequence under the best case of the system are

$$T_{min} = 34 \text{ for } I_1,$$
$$T_{min} = 17 \text{ for } I_2,$$
$$T_{min} = 24 \text{ for } I_3.$$

5. Conclusions

This paper has given a systematic method to model and analyze the performance of concurrent real time systems by means of timed Petri nets. The practical system is first modeled by TPN. Based on the TPN model, the system is analyzed to get the results which are helpful to the design and management of the system. The Petri net is a powerful tool to model and analyze a concurrent real time system, but for more complex large-scale concurrent real time systems, such as air traffic control systems, chemical plant control systems, nuclear power plant control systems and so on, the automatic or semiautomatic analytical tools must be developed.

References

[1] H. Genrich and K. Lautenbach, "The Analysis of Distributed Systems by Means of Predicate/Transition Nets", Proc. Semantics of Concurrent Computation, France, 1979 (Lect. Notes Comput. Sci., Vol. 70), Springer Verlag, New York, 1979, pp. 123-146.

[2] K. Voss, "Using Predicate/Transition Nets to Model and Analyze Distributed Database Systems", *IEEE Trans. Software Eng.* Vol. SE-6, No. 6, Nov. 1980, pp. 539-544.

[3] S. Yau and M. Caglayan, "Distributed Software System Design Representation Using Modified Petri Nets", *IEEE Trans. Software Eng.* Vol. SE-9, No. 6, Nov. 1983, pp. 733-745.

[4] P. Merlin and D. Farber, "Recoverability of Communication Protocols-Implications of Theoretical Study", *IEEE Trans. Commun.* Vol. COM-24, No. 9, Sept. 1976, pp. 1036-1043.

[5] M. Diaz, "Modelling and Analysis of Communication and Cooperation Protocols Using Petrinet Based Models", *Comput. Networks* Vol. 6, No. 6,

Dec. 1982, pp. 419-441.

[6] J. Ayache J, Courtiat and M. Diaz, "REBUS: A Fault Tolerant Distributed System for Industrial Real Time Control", *IEEE Trans. Comput*, Vol. C-31, No. 7, July 1982, pp. 637-647.

[7] J. Peterson, "Petri Nets", *ACM Comput. Surv.* Vol. 9, No. 3, Sept. 1977, pp. 223-252.

[8] T. Agerwala, "Putting Petri Nets to Work", *Computer* Vol. 12, No. 12, Dec. 1979, pp. 85-94.

[9] C. Ramchandani, "Analysis of Asynchronous Concurrent Systems by Petri Nets", Project MAC, TR-120, M. I. T., Cambridge, MA, 1974.

[10] J. Sifakis, "Performance Evaluation of Systems Using Nets", in *Net Theory and Applications* (Lect. Notes Comput. Sci., Vol. 84), Springer Verlag, Berlin, 1980, pp. 307-319.

[11] K. Garg, "An Approach to Performance Specification of Communication Protocols Using Petri Nets", Proc. 4th Distributed Comput. Syst. Conf., San Francisco, CA, May 1984, pp. 202-212.

[12] R. Razouk and C. Phelps, "Performance Analysis Using Timed Petri Nets", Proc. 1984 Int. Conf. on Parallel Processing, 1984, pp. 126-128.

[13] T. Murata, "Modelling and Analysis of Concurrent Systems", in: C. Vick et al. (eds.), *Handbook of Software Engineering*, Van Nostrand, New York, 1984, pp. 39-63.

[14] M. Molly, "Performance Modelling Using Stochastic Petri Nets", *IEEE Trans. Comput.* Vol. C-31, No. 9, Sept. 1982, pp. 913-917.

3

Petri 网：一种用于信息系统模拟的方法*

一、引言

建立模型是现代科学常用的一种研究手段,因为我们要研究的客观事物总是处于多种因素交错的复杂纷乱的状态,使人们在研究问题时面临难以解决的困难。如果按照科学研究的特定目的,建立一个能够反映客体的本质关系的模型,就可以通过对模型的研究获得关于原型客体的认识,从而避免了制造真实现象耗费的成本所带来的麻烦和危险。

Petri 网(Petri net)是信息流的抽象的、形式的模型。研究 Petri 网的性质、概念和技术,对于描述和分析系统——尤其是并发异步系统——中的控制和信息流是一个简单、自然和极有用的方法,其主要用途在于构造事件的系统模型。利用 Petri 网理论,可给出要研究的系统的数学模型;然后对 Petri 网进行分析,就可得到系统的结构和动态行为的有关信息,利用这些信息可对所研究的系统进行评价或做出改进。

---

* 定稿。发表于《自然》1989 年第 12 卷 12 期,第 883-889 页。

利用 Petri 网来构造一个系统的模型有如下 3 条优点。第一，由于用图形表示和表示方法的精确性质，系统经常是容易理解的。第二，使用 Petri 网理论可以分析系统的特性。在 Petri 网理论中包含着标识树（marking tree）和不变集合（invariant set）这样的分析工具，可在某些网结构和系统动态特性之间建立一些关系；同时，也使它适用于并发系统的验证工作。第三，由于可以使用自下而上的手段生成 Petri 网，就有可能按部就班地设计出特性已知或特性易于验证的系统来。[1]

Petri 网理论是联邦德国 IGMD 研究所（Institut für Informations systemforohung der Gesellschaft für Mathematik und Datenverarbeitung）的 C. A. Petri 教授在研究系统中的信息流的新模型时提出的，最早见于其 1962 年的博士学位论文。接着，Petri 网的思想引起了 A. D. R. J.（Applied Data Research Inc.）研究小组的注意，他们和麻省理工学院（MIT）一起对此做了进一步的发展，使得 Petri 网得到了广泛的传播，在各个领域得到了广泛的应用。[2] 到目前为止，Petri 网已被用于计算机各个领域的系统的形式描述、模拟、设计和分析：通讯协议[3-7]、分布式系统[8-12]、性能评价[13-18]、程序设计语言[19, 20]、操作系统[21]和编译系统（将 Petri 网应用于模拟编译程序，以确定现存的编译是否适合于并行处理[22]），以及计算机系统结构[23]等。在硬件设计方面，像 CDC6600 这样由多功能部件构成的计算机也已经模型化了——使用 Petri 网产生了高效率的 CDC6600 程序：把通常用高级语言表示的算法直接改用网表示，以消除使用高级语言所带来的顺序执行的限制，接着就将目标硬件所要求的顺序执行的限制引入网中，这个网所能执行的所有顺序都可在目标硬件上实现，并且能起到反映实在系统功能的良好作用。[1]另外，Petri 网在控制理论[24]、柔性制造系统 FMS[25, 26]，以及在社会科学领域中的法律方面[27, 28]都有应用，并取得了成果。

27

二、Petri 网

1. Petri 网的基本结构和图形表示

Petri 网为一有向图，具有两种结点：一是"位置"（place），用圆圈表示；二是"变迁"（transition），用直线段表示。位置的集合为 P，变迁的集合记为 T，则 Petri 网可形式地定义为

$$N = (P, T, A)。$$

其中，$P = \{p_1, p_2, \cdots, p_n\}$，$T = \{t_1, t_2, \cdots, t_m\}$，$A \subseteq P \times T \cup T \times P$，为结点间有向弧的集合，它规定了两种函数 I 和 O。对每个用 t_i 表示的变迁，函数 I 定义 t_i 的一组输入位置 $I(t_i)$，函数 O 定义 t_i 的一组输出位置 $O(t_i)$。若用 t_i 表示事件，则 $I(t_i)$ 表示该事件发生的条件，$O(t_i)$ 表示该事件发生的结果，这样的 Petri 网可用来表示系统的静态性质。图 1 是 Petri 网的一个例子。其中，

$$P = \{p_1, p_2, p_3, p_4, p_5\},$$
$$I(t_1) = \{p_1, p_5\},$$
$$I(t_2) = \{p_2\},$$
$$I(t_3) = \{p_3, p_5\},$$
$$I(t_4) = \{p_4\};$$
$$T = \{t_1, t_2, t_3, t_4\},$$
$$O(t_1) = \{p_2\},$$
$$O(t_2) = \{p_1, p_5\},$$
$$O(t_3) = \{p_4\},$$
$$O(t_4) = \{p_3, p_5\}。$$

为了使 Petri 网能动态地反映系统的特性，在位置中引入一些标志（token），用黑点表示。按照系统状态被赋予一定的标志分布的

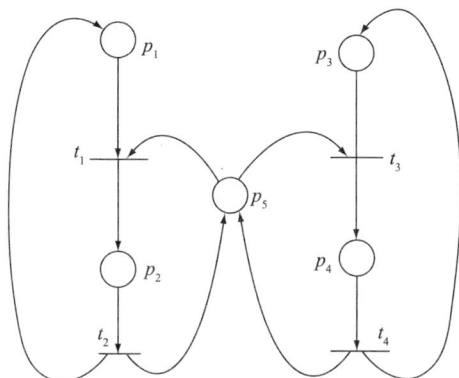

图 1　一个 Petri 网

Petri 网，通常称为"有标识的 Petri 网"（marked Petri net）。标志的分布情况，可以反映出系统状态随各事件发生而出现的变化。显然，由于系统状态的动态性质，Petri 网中的标志分布是时间的函数。

我们用 m_i 来表示位置 p_i 的标志数，则向量 $\boldsymbol{M} = (m_1, m_2, \cdots, m_n)$ 表示由 n 个位置所构成的 Petri 网的标识。图 2(a)是一个有标识的 Petri 网，其标识可写成

$$\boldsymbol{M} = (1, 0, 1, 0, 1)。$$

这样，为了描述 Petri 网的动态特性，可采用四元组 $\boldsymbol{N} = (\boldsymbol{P}, \boldsymbol{T}, \boldsymbol{A}, \boldsymbol{M})$ 来表示一个 Petri 网。

Petri 网的形式化表示和图形表示是等价的，即可从 Petri 网结构中得到 Petri 网图，反之亦然。

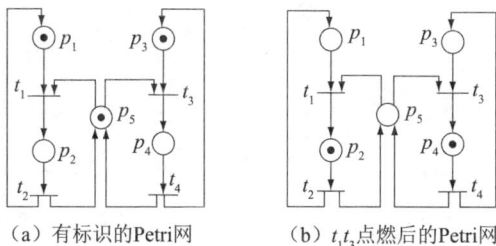

（a）有标识的Petri网　　　　（b）t_1t_3点燃后的Petri网

图 2　有标识的 Petri 网和变迁点燃

2. Petri 网的执行

Petri 网中变迁的点燃规则(firing rule)如下：

(1) 一个变迁是可行的(enabled)，是指它的每一个输入位置至少必须具备一个标志；

(2) 只有当变迁是可行的，该变迁才可以进行点燃；

(3) 当一个变迁进行点燃时，

i) 从每个输入位置移去一个标志，

ii) 在每个输出位置放入一个标志。

点燃变迁将会改变 Petri 网的标识 M。值得注意的是，只有可行的变迁才可以点燃。因此，当变迁点燃之后，网中的每个位置中的标志数保持非负，同时，标识即标志分布也相应地发生变化。如果变迁的输入位置中的标志数不够，则此变迁是不可行的，从而不能点燃。

对于图 2(a) 的 Petri 网，在这样的标识下，变迁 t_1 和 t_3 是可行的，而 t_2 和 t_4 是不可行的，因为 p_2 和 p_4 中都没有标志。图 2(b) 是 t_1 和 t_3 点燃后的 Petri 网，此时的标识 $M = (0, 1, 0, 1, 0)$。只要有可行的变迁，变迁的点燃就可继续进行，当没有可行的变迁时，执行停止。

顺便指出，图 1 实际上给出了互斥问题的 P/V 解法的 Petri 网模型。著名的 P、V 操作是为研究进程的同步和互斥而定义的，它对信号灯(semaphore) s (s 是一个整型变量)进行操作：

$$P(s)：当 s > 0，则 s := s - 1,$$
$$V(s)：s := s + 1。$$

这两个操作是不可分割的。只有当 s 为正值时，一个进程才能执行它的 P 操作，否则它就无法减 1 和继续下去。一个 V 操作就是简单地给 s 加1(以便允许其他进程执行 P 操作)。两个进程不能在同一个信号灯上同时执行 P 和 V 操作。例如，

进程 1	进程 2
P(mutax)	P(mutax)
互斥区	互斥区
V(mutax)	V(mutax)

这就是用 P 和 V 操作解决互斥问题的方法。信号灯 mutax 对两个进程是共用的，其初值为 1。从图 2 中可看出，p_2 和 p_4 是由 p_5 所控制的互斥事件。

三、 系统的 Petri 网模拟和分析

Petri 网模拟一系统时着重于系统的两个方面：事件（event）和条件（condition）以及它们之间的关系。从这个角度看，一个系统在任何给定的时间内，将具有某些条件，具有这些条件就会引起某一事件的发生；这些事件的发生可以改变系统的状态，从而造成原来的某些条件的消失，导致一些新的条件的出现。

我们以操作系统中著名的生产者—消费者问题（producer-consumer problem）为例子来说明 Petri 网模拟和分析的具体方法和步骤。[1] 由于所举的这个例子具有普遍性，因此这些方法就具有一般意义。

```
Semaphore E; initial (E)=B
Semaphore F; initial (F)=0
Semaphore M; initial (M)=1
Producer（生产者）:            Consumer（消费者）
PROD: "produce（生产）"       CONS: P(F)
       P(E)                          P(M)
       P(M)                          "从缓冲器中移去"
       "放入缓冲器"                  V(M)
       V(M)                          V(E)
       V(E)                          "consume（消费）"
       Go to PROD                    Go to CONS
```

图 3　使用 P 和 V 操作协调两个并发进程的程序

　　我们考虑由两个进程组成的生产者—消费者系统：①一个生产者(输入进程或设备)，它接收数据，并将其放在一个有限缓冲器中(大小为 B)；②一个消费者(计算性进程或设备)，它从缓冲器中取出数据，并且加以运算。这两个进程异步工作，但必须避免同时访问缓冲器，还必须避免缓冲器的上溢出和下溢出。图 3 给出了使用 P、V 操作来协调两个进程的程序。(E 表示缓冲器内空出的单元数，F 表示缓冲器中存有数据的单元数，M 被用来避免对缓冲器的存取冲突。)图 4 给出了表现该系统的简洁的 Petri 网。下面，作为系统验证的例子，将使用两种方法分析这个网。

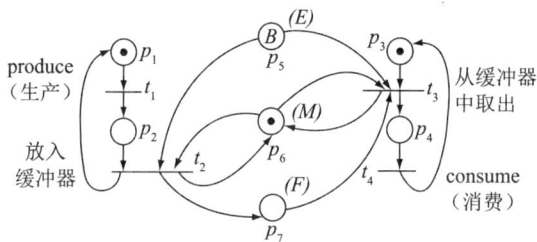

图 4　生产者—消费者系统的 Petri 网

　　在第一种方法中，使用网的不变集合。不变集合是一个位置集合 I，它使 $\sum_{p\in I} m(p)$ 对每个可达标识 M 是一个常数，且没有它的任何真子集是不变集合。令 $N = (T, P, A)$ 是一个 Petri 网。将 N 的关联矩阵 (incidence matrix) C 定义为 $C = (c(t, p))$，其中 $t\in T$ 且 $p\in P$，

$$c(t, p) = \begin{cases} -1, & \text{当}(p, t)\in A, (t, p)\notin A, \\ +1, & \text{当}(t, p)\in A, (p, t)\notin A, \\ 0, & \text{其他。} \end{cases}$$

　　设 Y 是下面方程组的一个解：

$$C \cdot Y = 0,$$

其中 Y 的每个元素是 0 或 1，且 Y 不可能由其他解的迭加而得到，即 Y 是线性方程组的基础解。与 Y 的非零元素相对应的位置的集合就是一个不变集合。[1]对于图 4 中的 Petri 网，上面的方程组成为

$$
\begin{array}{c}
t_1 \\
t_2 \\
t_3 \\
t_4
\end{array}
\begin{pmatrix}
p_1 & p_2 & p_3 & p_4 & p_5 & p_6 & p_7 \\
-1 & 1 & 0 & 0 & 0 & 0 & 0 \\
1 & -1 & 0 & 0 & -1 & 0 & 1 \\
0 & 0 & -1 & 1 & 1 & 0 & -1 \\
0 & 0 & 1 & -1 & 0 & 0 & 0
\end{pmatrix}
\cdot
\begin{pmatrix}
y_1 \\
y_2 \\
y_3 \\
y_4 \\
y_5 \\
y_6 \\
y_7
\end{pmatrix}
=
\begin{pmatrix}
0 \\
0 \\
0 \\
0 \\
0 \\
0 \\
0
\end{pmatrix}。
$$

即得到如下的联立线性方程组：

$$
\begin{cases}
-y_1 + y_2 = 0, \\
y_1 - y_2 - y_5 - y_7 = 9, \\
-y_3 + y_4 + y_5 - y_7 = 0, \\
y_3 - y_4 = 0。
\end{cases}
$$

它的不能由其他解迭加而得的解是

$$(1, 1, 0, 0, 0, 0, 0),$$
$$(0, 0, 0, 0, 1, 0, 1),$$
$$(0, 0, 1, 1, 0, 0, 0),$$
$$(0, 0, 0, 0, 0, 1, 0),$$

不变集合是

$$\{p_1, p_2\}, \{p_3, p_4\}, \{p_5, p_7\}, \{p_6\}。$$

　　从得到的不变集合就可以推断出网的某些动态性质。假设初始标识 M_0 如图 4 所画出的那样，即 $M_0 = (1, 0, 1, 0, 0, 1, 0)$，且 $B > 0$；又设 N_{p_i} 表示在 p_i 中标志的总数。

　　有界性（boundedness）：因为每个位置都位于某个不变集合中，

而且该网由一个有界标识开始，所以这个网是有界的。

守恒性（conservativeness）：位置的集合可以划分为一些互不相交的子集，其中的每个子集都是不变集合，所以该网是守恒的，即在该网中的标志总数保持常数。

互斥性（mutual exclusion）：如果一变迁 t 的输入或输出位置包含在不变集合 I 中，则称 t 为 I 的变迁。如果两个变迁都是同一不变集合的变迁，且它们的初始标识使得在不变集合中的位置内的标志总数是 1，则称这两个变迁是互斥的，是不能同时点燃的。在图 4 中，初始标识和不变集合 $\{p_6\}$ 就保证了 t_2 和 t_3 是互斥的。

缓冲器无下溢（no buffer underflow）：缓冲器下溢是不可能的，因为当缓冲器是空的（$N_{p_7}=0$）时，t_3 是不可点燃的。

缓冲器无上溢（no buffer overflow）：由于 $\{p_5, p_7\}$ 是不变集合，初始标识保证了 $N_{p_5}+N_{p_7}$ 总是 B，因此，$N_{p_7}\leqslant B$，不可能出现缓冲器上溢的现象。

无死锁（no deadlock）：如果一个网到达了所有变迁都不可点燃的标识，则称该网是死锁的。若图 4 中的网是死锁的，则 t_2 不能点燃。这意味着，$N_{p_5}=0$ 或 $N_{p_2}=0$。在前一种情形中，从初始标识 M_0 和不变集合 $\{p_5, p_7\}$ 可以得到 $N_{p_7}>0$；若 $N_{p_3}=0$，则 $N_{p_4}=1$（由不变集合 $\{p_3, p_4\}$ 知），且 t_4 是可点燃的，否则 $N_{p_3}=1$，且 t_3 是可点燃的。在后一种情形中，$N_{p_3}=0$，由不变集合 $\{p_1, p_2\}$ 和 M_0 可以得到 $N_{p_1}=1$，且 t_1 是可点燃的。于是，若 t_2 不可点燃，则 t_4、t_3 或 t_1 之一可点燃，故该网绝无死锁。

不变集合是验证 Petri 网特性的有用手段。无须特意去求解线性方程组，只要在构造 Petri 网的过程中遵循某些规则，就可以系统地得到全部不变集合。[29]

分析 Petri 网的另一基本手段是使用可达树（reachability tree）。一个标识 Petri 网的可达树的结点表示该网的可达标记。设 $N =$

$(T，P，A，M_0)$ 是一标识 Petri 网，且设 ω 是一特定量，对任何整数 x 都有 $\omega \pm x = \omega$，$x < \omega$ 和 $\omega \geqslant \omega$。M 在下面看作一个向量。N 的可达树可按下述方法构造。

Begin

设初始结点是根结点，且给它标上"new"标签。

While 带"new"标签的标识存在 do。

选择一个带有"new"标签的标识 M。

如果 M 等同于树中标签不是"new"的其他结点，则给 M 带上"old"标签且停止处理 M。

如果在 M 中再有变迁是可行的，则给 M 带上"终结"的标签。

对于 M 中的每个可行变迁 t，得到标识 M'，它是由点燃 M 中的变迁 t 而产生的。

如果存在从根到 M 的路径，它包含着标识 M'' 使 $M' > M''$，则对 $(M')_i > (M'')_i$ 的 i 都用 ω 替代 $(M')_i$。

引进 M' 作为一个结点，从 M 到 M' 画一条弧，并标以标号 t，且给 M' 带上"new"标签。

End

可以看出，上面的过程总能在有限步内结束，并产生一棵有限树。同时，一位置 p_i 是无界的，当且仅当这棵树包含着一个具有 $(M)_i = \omega$ 的标识。对于有界网，每个结点都是一可达标识，并且该树包含着所有的可达标识。图 5 给出了图 4 Petri 网在 $B = 1$ 时的可达树。对这棵树的分析产生了一些有用的信息。它确切地给出了可达标识的集合。因为没有任何结点包含着 ω，故该网是有界的。该网也是守恒的：在每个标识中的标志数目之和都是 4。不存在缓冲器上溢，因为任何标识都不给 p_7 分配两个以上的标志，同时也无缓冲器下溢现象。对这棵树的分析指出，从该树中的任何标识开始，对每一个变迁都可以用一适当的点燃序列使其成为可行的；也就是说，该网是活的，无死锁现象。若令 $B=1$，则 t_2 和 t_3 绝不可能同时可行，因此它们是互斥的。从对可达树的分析中，可以得到关于系统特性的详细信息。

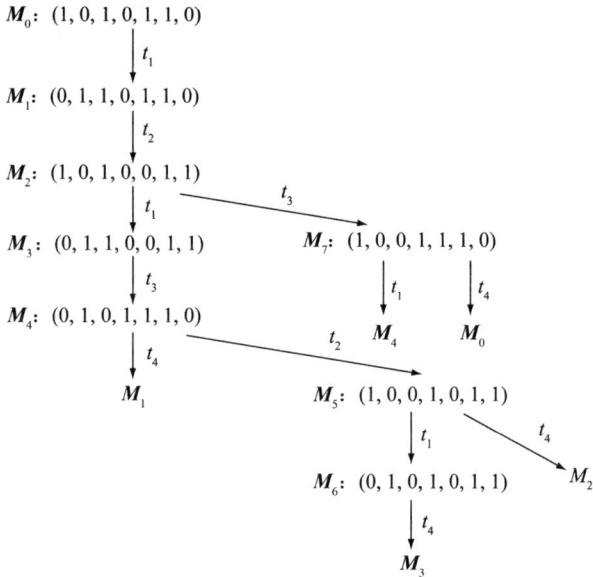

图 5　图 4 的 Petri 网在 $B=1$ 时的可达树

较复杂的系统也可以用 Petri 网建立模型。考察一个由以下几部分组成的计算机系统：处理机、输入表、输出表和作业。其操作如下：①作业进入系统并放入输入表，当处理机空闲并且在输入表中有作业时，处理机立即开始处理这个作业；②当作业处理完毕后就把它放入输出表；③如果输入表上有更多的作业，则处理机继续处理其他作业，否则处理机处于等待的空闲状态。

这个系统的模型可以用图 6 中的 Petri 网进行描述。注意到位置 p_1 中有 4 个标志，说明有 4 个作业进入系统等待处理；p_2 中有一个标志，说明有一个处理机是空闲的。如果允许在位置 p_2 中有多个标志出现,那么就可以模拟多处理机系统的行为了。

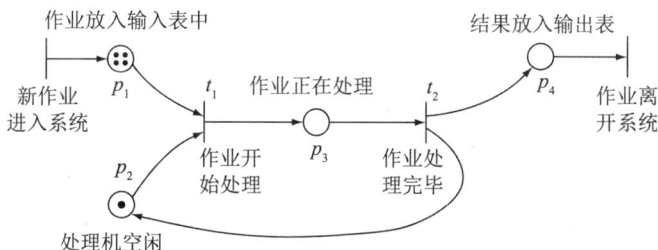

图 6　一个计算机系统的 Petri 网模型

四、 Petri 网的子类和扩充

任何模型的成功都有两个因素:它的模拟能力和它的判定能力。模拟能力指正确表现所模拟系统的能力,使模型忠实地代表所模拟的系统;判定能力指分析该系统的特定形式以及确定所模拟系统的性质的能力。

这两个因素一般应同时兼顾。Petri 网模型代表一种在这两个因素之间进行折中的尝试。它们具有比有限状态模型更好的模拟能力,而同时保留了后者大部分的判定能力。事实上,Petri 网起初就是被确定来回答有限状态模型的受限制的模拟能力的。[2]

1. Petri 网的子类

人们希望对 Petri 网的模拟能力(相对于图灵机来讲)施加一些限制而使其在判定能力方面得到一些提高。其结果就变成去定义许多 Petri 网的子类,希望从中找到一个具有已知的判定能力且仍旧对实际用途保持适当的模拟能力的子类。对这些子类的确定,都是对其结构进行限制以增进其可分析性。

最经常被考虑的两个子类是状态机和标记图。状态机对 Petri

网施加的限制是：每一个变迁恰好有一个输入和一个输出。实际上，它们恰好是有限状态自动机类。既为有限，有限状态自动机必有很高的判定能力。然而，当被用来模拟非有限的系统时，它们的作用是有限制的。标记图是状态机的对偶，它也被广泛地研究过。一个标记图也是一种 Petri 网，它的每一个位置恰好有一个输入变迁和一个输出变迁，表明标记图是活的和安全的以及求解标记图的可达性问题的算法都已经知道了。标记图有较高的判定能力，但它们只有有限的模拟能力，因为它们只能模拟那些其控制流没有分支的系统。换言之，它们能够容易地模拟并发的活跃性，但不能模拟交替的活跃性。[2]

2. Petri 网的扩充

一种显而易见的扩充方法是，去掉一位置在一次变迁点燃中只移去或放入一个标志的限制。试考察化学反应的模拟。[2]这里，一个位置中的一个标志代表一个确实的分子或原子的可利用性，用变迁来模拟化学反应，而且每当标志表明反应物可用时就可以发生反应，变迁的点燃用来模拟反应。它花掉了输入标志（反应物），并产生了输出标志（生成物）。要想表示一化学反应可能需要不止一个单位的化学反应，就要在诸变迁与诸位置之间使用多重有向弧来模拟所必需的标志数。图 7 给出了需要 3 个 Cl_2 与 2 个 P 以产生 2 个 PCl_2 的化学反应的 Petri 网模型。为了使变迁点燃，至少有 3 个 Cl_2 和 2 个 P 可使用才行。变迁的点燃吸收掉这些标志，并在它的输出位置上产生两个标志。允许使用多重弧线的 Petri 网是一种广义上的 Petri 网——加权 Petri 网。

近年来的研究表明，由于长期以来 Petri 网没有考虑时间因素，而其所模拟的系统对象又往往是与时间有关联的，因此不易被作为性能分析的工具，致使其应用范围受到了严重限制。时间 Petri 网（timed Petri net）和随机 Petri 网（stochastic Petri net）的提出正好弥补了这种不足，使人们能够对模型系统进行更为有效的分析和评价。

人们以各种方式把时间引入 Petri 网。一是每个位置关联一个时

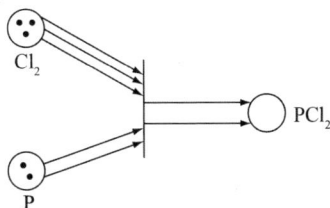

图7　化学反应的 Petri 网模型

间参数，二是每个变迁关联一个时间参数。目前大多数采用后者，这是因为 Petri 网作为一种系统的模型，一个事件在系统中的发生（通常用一个变迁的点燃来表示）需要一定的时间，因此时间与变迁相关联是自然的。这表明，变迁成为可行的之后尚需经过一定的时间才能点燃，即变迁的点燃需要一定的时间，也称为变迁点燃延时（transition firing delays）。但就网的分析而言，这两种方式是等价的。[13]

　　在实际的模型设计中，变迁与时间之间的关联可以有确定的或随机的两种方式。在确定的方式下，相关于每个变迁的时间被定义成一个常数，以这种方式扩展成的 Petri 网称为时间 Petri 网。[13, 18, 30]在随机的方式下，每个变迁点燃延时被定义为一个随机变批，具有给定的概率分布，以这种方式扩展成的 Petri 网称为随机 Petri 网。[15, 31-36]

五、结束语

　　Petri 网作为一种系统的形式模型，提供了一种直观、简明、有力的分析工具，能对系统的有界性、守恒性、可覆盖性以及标识的可达性等特性进行全面的分析，已在各个领域得到了广泛的应用。然而，有些性质，例如两个 Petri 网的包含性或等价性问题，与希尔伯特（Hilbert）的第十问题一样，已被指明是不可判定的。[37]即使有些是可判定的，在一些情况下其时空复杂性也相当大，例如对于第三节所给出的例子，当取 $B > 1$ 时，可达树就会变得复杂起来。Petri 网的一些子类虽然也具备很好的判定性，但对于有用的模拟来讲似乎还有限制。这些问题以及与 Petri 网有关的其他许多课题，都有待进一步的研究。

参考文献

[1] Agerwala T., *Computer* 12, 12 (1979) 85.

[2] Peterson J. L., *ACM Computing Surveys* 9, 3 (1977) 223.

[3] Merlin P., *IEEE Trans. Comp*. 24, 6 (1976) 1036.

[4] Diaz M., *Computer Networks* 6, 6 (1982) 419.

[5] Bertholtt G., Terrat R., *IEEE Trans. Commun*. 30, 12 (1982) 2497.

[6] Garg K., *IEEE Trans. Soft. Eng*. 11, 10 (1985) 1216.

[7] 姚毓林,微电子学与计算机, 6, 1 (1989) 1.

[8] 姚毓林, *Proc. of Int. Conf. on System Simulation and Scientific Computing* (1989).

[9] Genrich H., Lautenbach K., *Semantics of Concurrent Computing*, Hahned G. ed., Springer Verlag (1979) 123.

[10] Voss K., *IEEE Trans. Soft. Eng*. 6, 6 (1980) 539.

[11] Ayache J. et al., *IEEE Trans. Comp*. 31, 7 (1982) 637.

[12] Yau S., Caglayan M., *IEEE Trans. Soft. Eng*. 9, 6 (1983) 733.

[13] Sifakis J., *Net Theory and Applications*, Brauer W. ed., Springer Verlag (1980) 307.

[14] Ramamoorthy C. V., Ho G. S., *IEEE Trans. Soft. Eng*. 6, 5 (1980) 440.

[15] Molly M., *IEEE Trans. Comp*. 31, 9 (1982) 913.

[16] Magott J., *Information Processing Letters* 18 (1984) 7.

[17] Murata T., *Handbook of Software Engineering*, Vick C. ed. (1984) 39.

[18] Razouk R., Phelps C., *Proc. of 1984 Int. Conf. on Parallel Processing* (1984) 126.

[19] Lauer P. E. et al., *Acta Informatica* 12 (1979) 109.

[20] Kluge W. E. et al., *IEEE Trans. Soft. Eng*. 9, 4 (1983) 415.

[21] Noe J., *Proc. of ACM SIGOPS Workshop on System Performance Evaluation ACM* (1971) 362.

[22] Baer J. L., Ellis C. S., *IEEE Trans. Soft. Eng*. 3, 6 (1977) 394.

[23] Chen T., "Introduction to Computer Architecture", Stone H. ed., *Science Research Associates* (1975) 375.

[24] Murata T., *IEEE Trans. Auto. Cont*. 22, 3 (1977) 412.

[25] Martinez J. et al., Modelling and Design of Flexible Manufacturing Systems,

Kusiak A. ed., *Elseviel Sci. Pub. B. V*. (1986) 389.

[26] Alla H. et al., Modelling and Design of Flexible Manufacturing Systems, Kusiak A. ed., *Elseviel Sci. Pub. B. V*. (1986) 271.

[27] Meldman J., Holt A., *Jurimetrics J*. 12, 2 (1971) 65.

[28] Meldman J., J. *Law and Tech*. 19, 2 (1978) 121.

[29] Agerwala T. et al., *Proc. 15th Design Automation Conf*. Las Vegas (1978) 305.

[30] Zuberek W., *Proc. 7th Annu. Symp. Computer Architecture* (1980) 88.

[31] Marsan M. et al., *ACM Trans. Comp*. 12, 2 (1984) 93.

[32] Dugan J. et al., *Proc. of 10th Int. Symo. Models of Comp. Syst. Performance* (1984) 507.

[33] Molloy M., *IEEE Trans. Soft. Eng*. 11, 4 (1985) 417.

[34] Balbo G. et al., *IEEE Trans. Soft. Eng*. 12, 4 (1986) 561.

[35] Holliday M., Vernon M., *IEEE Trans. Soft. Eng*. 13, 12 (1987) 1297.

[36] Holliday M., Vernon M., *IEEE Trans. Comp*. 36, 1 (1987) 76.

[37] 殷兆麟，计算机研究与发展，20, 10 (1983) 1.

4

基于 Hopfield 神经网络模型的启发式学习算法及其在数字模式处理中的应用*

一、引言

传统的 Von Neumann 计算机发展至今，已不能满足日益增长的高速计算以及实时语言识别、视觉与机器人等机器感知处理的需求。一方面，在总结前四代计算机科学技术的基础上，结合人工智能技术手段，试图用第五代计算机来解决矛盾。另一方面，神经生理方面的专家长期以来对大脑神经的研究，大大地促进了试图用大量并行的简单电子单元来模拟神经网络功能的设想。尤其是自 20 世纪 80 年代以来，由于 Hopfield 的突破性工作[1-4]，使得人工神经网络（在不混淆的情况下，简称"神经网络"）在联想记忆、优化计算、并行分布式处理、专家系统、机器感知、智能控制和机器人控制等领域得到了广泛的应用，提出了一些新的方法，并解决了一些难题。神经网络很容易由 VLSI 实现，这更使其发展有着良好的前景。

神经网络是由许多并行运行的简单神经元（处理单元）组成的系统，其处理能力由网络的结构、连接强度（权值）以及单个神经元所执

---

* 定稿。第一作者为笔者，共同作者为张逸敏、洪进。发表于《机器人》（中国自动化学会）第 12 卷第 4 期，1990 年第 21 - 24 页。

行的处理决定。Hopfield 网以大规模并行处理的方式进行,网络不断地学习和自适应,直至达到目标为止。本文给出了一个基于 Hopfield 神经网络模型的启发式学习算法,并完成了在计算机中的实现,进而运用算法对一些被 0.1 和 0.25 随机噪声干扰的数学模型进行了校正处理,得到了较好的结果。

二、神经网络模型

1. 神经元的数学描述

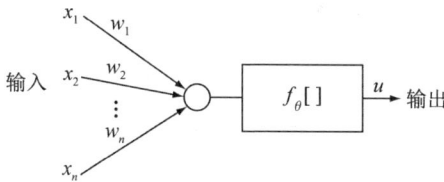

图 1 神经元功能的数学描述

一个神经元可以被看作一个多输入、单输出的具有阈值非线性特性的部件(图 1)。设神经元有 n 个输入 x_1, x_2, $\cdots$, x_n,这些输入可能是上一级神经元的输出,也可能是本级神经元的反馈,我们使用一个 n 维向量 $\boldsymbol{X} = (x_1, x_2, \cdots, x_n)$ 来表示。每个输入通过一个突触(synapse)联系系数 W_i($i = 1, 2, \cdots, n$)作用于该神经元。神经元对这些输入进行时空总和后送到一个阈值非线性元件 $f_\theta[\ ]$。$f_\theta[\ ]$ 可以是一个阶跃函数:

$$f_\theta[x] = \begin{cases} 1, & \text{当 } x \geqslant \theta \text{ 时,} \\ 0, & \text{当 } x < \theta \text{ 时,} \end{cases}$$

其中,θ 是阈值。最后,由 $f_\theta[\ ]$ 给出神经元的输出 u。

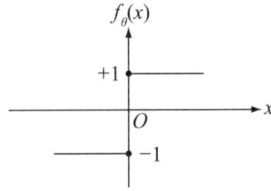

图 2 $f_\theta(x)$ 函数

2. 神经网络模型和 Hebb 学习规则

设有 N 个神经元互相连接。每个神经元的活性状态 u_i（$i=1$，2，$\cdots$，n）只能取 -1 或 1 分别代表抑制与兴奋。其状态按下述规律变化：

$$u_i = f_\theta \left[\sum_j t_{ij} u_j - \theta_i \right]; \; i = 1, 2, \cdots, n, \qquad (1)$$

其中，t_{ij} 是神经元间的连接强度的权值，$t_{ii}=0$，学习过程就是调节 t_{ij} 的过程。（1）式称为一个神经网络模型。

Hebb 规则[5]就是调节 t_{ij} 的原则，即若第 i 与第 j 个神经元同时处于兴奋状态，则它们之间的连接应加强，即

$$\Delta t_{ij} = \alpha u_i u_j (\alpha > 0)。$$

这一规则与巴甫洛夫的条件反射学说一致，并已得到神经网络学说的证明。[6]

3. Hopfield 模型

Hopfield 神经网络模型由 N 个神经元组成，在上一节神经网络中的 $f_\theta(x)$ 取为 $f_h(x)$：

$$f_h(x) = \begin{cases} 1, & x \geqslant 0, \\ -1, & x < 0, \end{cases} \qquad (2)$$

如图 2 所示。神经元的状态随机地异步变化：

$$u_i = \begin{cases} 1, & \sum\limits_{i \neq 1} t_{ij} u_j - \theta_i \geq 0, \\ & \qquad\qquad\qquad\qquad 0 \leq i, j \leq N-1, \quad (3) \\ -1, & \sum\limits_{i \neq 1} t_{ij} u_j - \theta_i < 0, \end{cases}$$

u_i，t_{ij} 和 θ_i 的含义同上一节。Hopfield 模型的神经网络结构参见图 3。

三、 基于 Hopfield 模型的启发式算法

Hopfield 网络[1-4, 7] 可被用于联想式记忆（associative memory），本文考虑其内容相关记忆（content-addressable memory）的特性，即从部分信息中获得完整信息。

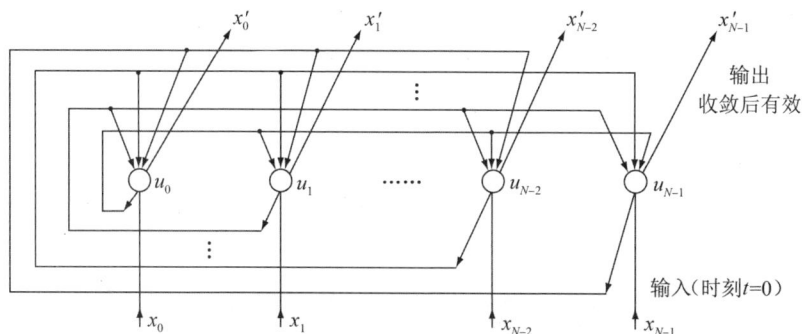

图 3　内容相关记忆的 Hopfield 神经网络结构

图 3 给出了有 N 个结点的具有内容相关记忆的 Hopfield 神经网络，函数 $f_\theta [\ ]$ 取值同（2）式，网络的二值输入输出取 +1 和 -1。每个结点的输出通过权 t_{ij} 反馈到其他所有的结点上。图 4 给出了这个基于 Hopfield 模型的启发式算法。算法由所有类别的样本模式设置网的连接权值 t_{ij} 开始，这是一个 $N \times N$ 的矩阵。然后从图像中直接读入需要的输入模式并初始化有关向量。利用上节给出的（2）式对输入模式在离散的时间步长 t 上进行循环操作。循环的收敛判据

是连续两次循环的输出完全一致。在网络收敛的结点输出就是网络的输出。

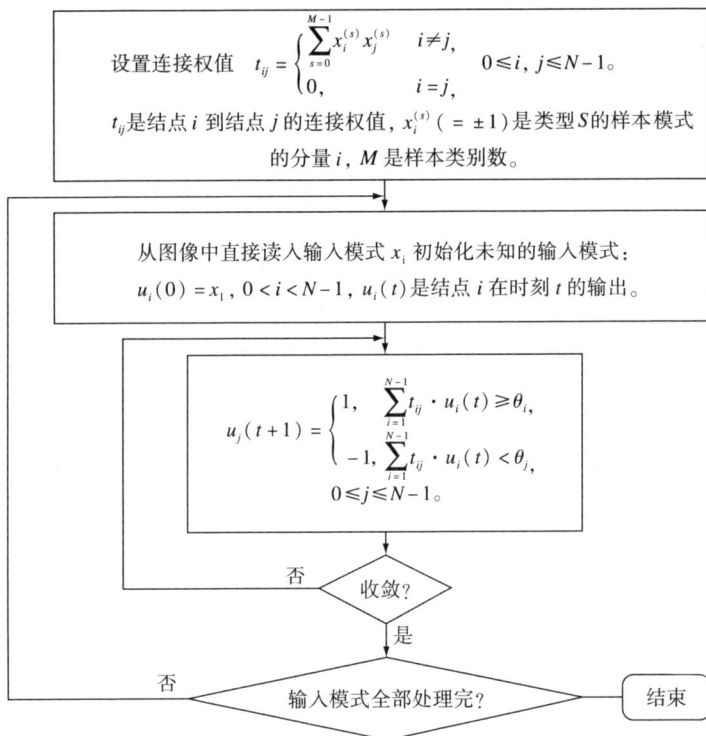

图 4　基于 Hopfield 模型的启发式算法

Hopfield[2]和 Cohen[8]等证明了，如果加权对称且结点是异步更新的，则网络必收敛。

四、算法应用及实验结果

上述算法具有内容相关记忆的特性，即可从部分信息中获得完整信息。考察计算机图像处理时校正（或恢复）被噪声干扰的图像的过程，实质上可以被看成一个从部分信息中推得完整信息的过程。

图 5(b)(c)的最左边一列模式分别被随机噪声所干扰。对于(c)中的最左边列的数学模式,从整体上已难以辨认,但它仍保留原图像的部分信息。根据上节给出的启发式算法的内容相关记忆的特性,可以从被干扰的数字模式(含有部分信息)经过算法处理恢复到原来清晰的数字模式(拥有全部信息)。

(a) 6个样本数字模式

(b) 噪声干扰为0.1时,数字"1""2"和"4"的输出　　　(c) 噪声干扰为0.25时,数字"1""2"和"4"的输出

图 5　算法对具有 6 个数字的模式集合的处理

在上节给出的神经网络中,我们取神经元个数 $N = 120$,从而有 14 400 个权被训练,使之能校正和恢复被噪声干扰的模式。权值不断改变的过程也就是不断进行启发式学习的过程。图中每个黑白二值的数字模式含有 $12 \times 10 = 120$(个)像素点。模式输入时,黑点像素取值 $+1$,白点像素取值 -1。图 5(b)(c)分别给出了算法对被随机噪声 0.1 和 0.25 干扰的数字模式"0""2"和"4"进行处理的结果。从图中可以看出,算法分别经过几次循环即可成功校正被噪声干扰的数字模式,使之恢复到原样本的数字模式。

五、结论

本文给出了一个基于 Hopfield 神经网络的启发式内容相关联想

的学习算法。运用这个算法对 6 个分别被 0.1 和 0.25 随机噪声干扰的数字模式成功地进行了校正处理,得到了较好的结果。但是,Hopfield 网络有其自身的局限性,在 $M > 0.15N$ 时,输入模式有可能收敛到与所有样本模式都不相同的模式;而在 $M < 0.15N$ 时,这种情况极少出现。[1]另外,我们在实验中发现,样本模式之间的共同像素点应尽量少,否则可能使得收敛不能得到预期的结果。

参考文献

[1] Hopfield J. J., "Neural Network and Physical System with Emergent Collective Computational Abilities", *Proc. Natl. Arad. Sci. USA*, 1982; 79: 2554-2558.

[2] Hopfield J. J., "Neurons with Graded Response Have Collective Computational Properties Like Those of Two-state Neurons", *Proc. Natl. Arad. Sci. USA*, 1984; 81: 3088-3092.

[3] Hopfield J. J., Tank D. W., "Neural Computation of Decision in Optimization Problem", *Biol. Cybern.*, 1985; 52: 142-152.

[4] Hopfield J. J., Tank D. W., "Computing with Neural Circuits: A Model", *Science*, 1986; 233: 625-633.

[5] Hebb D, O., *The Organization of Behavior*. John Wiley & Sons, New York, 1949.

[6] Kandel E, R., *Science*, 1982; 218: 433-443.

[7] Lippmann R, P., "An Introduction to Computing with Neural Nets", *IEEE ASSP Magazine*, 1987; 4 (2): 4-22.

[8] Cohen M. A., Grossberg S., "Absolute Stability of Global Patten Formation and Parallel Memory Storage by Competitive Neural Networks", *IEEE Trans Syst Man Cybern*, 1983; 13: 815-826.

5

A Petri Net Model for Temporal Knowledge Representation and Reasoning[①]

1. Introduction

In recent years, the increasing need for reasoning about time in various areas of artificial intelligence applications has led researchers to propose mainly two kinds of representation and reasoning schemes for temporal information: Dechter's linear inequalities[5, 6, 13] to encode metric relations between time points and Allen's temporal calculus. [1, 24] As Kautz stated in[11], each scheme has certain advantages. Linear inequalities can represent dates, durations, and other quantitative information that appears in real-world planning and scheduling problems. Allen's qualitative calculus can express certain crucial relations between time intervals, such as disjointedness, which cannot be expressed by any collection of simple linear inequalities (without specifying which intervals are before the other). In order to benefit

① Final submission version. *IEEE Transactions on Systems, Man and Cybernetics* Vol. 24, No. 9, September 1994, pp. 1374–1382. Submitted in January 1993; revised in May 1993 and October 1993.

from the advantages of each scheme, Kautz and Ladkin[11] have introduced a model to integrate two schemes for temporal reasoning. It consists of two parts: a metric network L_M and an Allen style network L_A. The L_M and L_A are kept separately. One has to translate information between L_M and L_A using the translation algorithms proposed in [11] to solve the reasoning tasks in their model. Meiri[14] has combined both qualitative and quantitative constraints into a unified network. However, it is difficult for both models to represent higher-order expression and repeated activities. Deng and Chang[7] have used Petri net to model both semantic and control knowledge, while Chen et al.[3] have presented a fuzzy Petri net model to represent the fuzzy production rules of a rule-based system, where the rule describes the fuzzy relation between two propositions. However, both models did not consider any temporal relation.

In this paper we present a general model based on Time Petri Net (henceforth TPN) for handling both qualitative and quantitative temporal information. In this model we are able to solve several representation and reasoning tasks. Specifically:

(1) Both metric relations between time points and qualitative relations between time interval can be encoded in a TPN model, which provides answers to many queries.

(2) We are able to express a higher-order expression such as "Tom drives to work at least 30 minutes more than Fred works" (see [6]).

(3) The model has an ability to represent repeated activities, such as "Tom goes to school every day", which constitute a large part of

the normal schedule (see [12]).

(4) The model is suitable for representing dynamic objects (especially concurrent activities), since Petri net itself is a good model for describing parallelism, nondeterminism and asynchronous characteristics.

(5) Each transition can be easily associated with a stochastical distributed random variable or a certainty factor to represent and solve uncertain tasks (more detail see [26]).

(6) Graphical representation of TPN gives a straightforward view of relations between objects, for example, disjunctive, compared to Allen's scheme in [1].

2. Basic Notions of Time Petri Net

Petri net theory is a graphical and modeling tool applicable to many fields. [2, 9, 15, 17, 19, 21, 27-30] The concept of time is not explicitly given in the original definition of Petri nets. Two basic Petri net-based models for handling time have been developed in the last 15 years, time Petri nets[16] and timed Petri nets[20]. Ramchandani's timed Petri nets[20] are derived from Petri net by associating a firing finite duration with each transition of the net. The classical firing rule of Petri net is modified first to account for the time it takes to fire a transition and second to express that a transition must fire as soon as it is enabled. These nets and related models have been used mainly for performance evaluation. Merlin's time Petri nets (TPN) are more general than timed Petri nets: a timed Petri net can be modeled by using a TPN, but the converse is not true. TPN's have been proved very convenient for expressing most of the temporal constraints while some of these constraints were difficult to express only in terms of durations. Berthmieu, Menasche, Diaz and other researchers at LAAS (Toulouse, France)[2, 15] proposed an enumerative analysis method which is related to reachability analysis for ordinary Petri nets. This technique allows one to simultaneously model and analyze the timed systems.

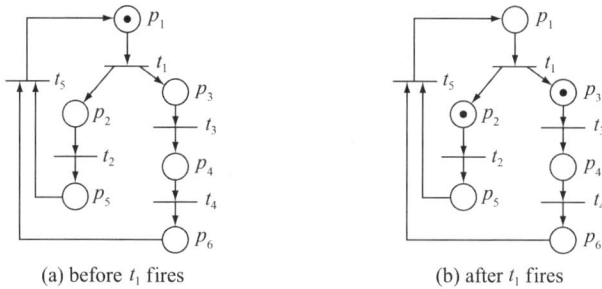

(a) before t_1 fires (b) after t_1 fires

Fig. 1 An example of Petri net

There are different definitions and terminology of Petri nets and TPN. The notations used in this paper follow that of [2, 15, 16] and [19].

Definition 1: A time Petri net is a tuple (P, T, B, F, M_0, *SIM*) *where*

- *P is a finite nonempty set of places p_i;*
- *T is a finite nonempty set of transitions t_i;*
- *B is the backward incidence function $B: T \times P \rightarrow N$, where N is the set of nonnegative integers;*
- *F is the forward incidence function $B: T \times P \rightarrow N$;*
- *M_0 is the initial marking function $M_0: P \rightarrow N$, (P, T, B, F and M_0 together define a Petri net);*
- *SIM is a mapping called static interval SIM: $T \rightarrow Q^* \times$*

$(Q^* \cup \infty)$, *where* Q^* *is the set of nonnegative rational numbers.*

A graph structure is often used for illustration of Petri net where a circle "O" represents a place and a bar "|" represents a transition. Fig. 1 shows a Petri net graph. An arrow from a place to a transition defines the place to be an input to the transition. Similarly, an output place is indicated by an arrow from the transition to the place.

The dynamic aspects of Petri net model are denoted by markings which are assignments of tokens ("." in the graph) to the places of a Petri net. The execution of a Petri net is controlled by the number and distribution of tokens in the Petri net. A transition is enabled if and only if each of its input places contains at least as many tokens as there exist arcs from that place to the transition. When a transition is enabled, it may fire. When a transition fires, all enabling tokens are removed from its input places, and a token is deposited in each of its output places. Given the Petri net marking in Fig. 1 (a), the next state after firing transition t_1 is shown in Fig. 1 (b). Transition firings continue as long as there exists at least one enabled transition.

In a TPN, two time values, which are two nonnegative rational numbers, a (called static Earliest Firing Time, static EFT for short) and b (called static Latest Firing Time, static LFT for short), with $a \leqslant b$, are associated with each transition. Assuming that any transition, e.g., t is being continuously enabled after it has been enabled,

• a $(0 \leqslant a)$, is the minimal time that must elapse, starting from the time at which transition t is enabled, until this transition can fire, and

• b $(0 \leqslant b \leqslant \infty)$, denoted the maximum time during which transition t can be enabled without being fired.

Times a and b for transition t, are relative to the moment at which transition t is enabled. Assuming the transition t has been enabled at time τ, then t, even if it is continuously enabled, cannot fire before time $\tau + a$ and must fire before or at time $\tau + b$; unless it is disabled before its firing by the firing of another transition.

The description of firing rule and the state in a TPN will be given in section 4, since they closely relate the dynamic behavior of a TPN.

It is easily to implement the computer representation of a Petri net, and then to simulate the dynamic behavior of the net (if one has defined the firing rule) and analyze the properties of the net. There have already been many powerful Petri nets software tools and packages on different platforms. An excellent review paper in this field can be found in [22].

For more than ten years, a group of researchers at France have been developing and using a Petri net-like graphical tool: Grafcet. In late 1980s, the Grafcet became an international standard IEC (International Electrotechnical Commission) 848 named "Preparation of Function Charts for Control Systems". The Grafcet is designed to describe the functioning of logic controllers. The main contribution of the Grafcet compared with the Petri nets is clear modeling of inputs and outputs and of their relations. [4, 23] It is admitted that the Grafcet allows easier and shorter description than Petri nets. Also the Grafcet can be more easily connected to the physical process, because translators and schedulers exist on programmable controllers. [8] However, there are two advantages of Petri nets over the Grafcet.

Firstly, Petri nets are better suited for mathematical and structural analysis. Secondly, in Grafcet model, at one time, all the firable transition fires. So this model evolves on a synchronous mode. First advantage is important for our model because the mathematical and structural analysis methods have great potential for reasoning (see Section 5). Second advantage is essential because the Petri nets have much more expressive power (this is decisive since our model must have ability of representing disjunctive cases, see Section 3).

3. TPN Representation

The main objective in this section is to express metric and interval temporal information using a TPN. We also discuss the TPN representation of higher-order expression and repeated activities.

As stated in [6], the primitive entities in the knowledge base are propositions or event with which we normally associate temporal intervals, e. g., "I read the newspaper"; each interval representing the time period during which the corresponding proposition holds. The temporal information might be relative (e. g., "I read the newspaper before I have breakfast"), or metric (e. g., "I take $30\sim40$ minutes to read the newspaper before have a 30-minute breakfast"). Both temporal information will be represented by a TPN in this section.

A. Dechter's Metric Information

By the definition of a TPN, it is easy to see that the metric temporal information [5], [6] can be naturally represented by a TPN. In this subsection we will use three examples to illustrate how to express, using a TPN, the metric constraints.

Let us consider the following examples:

- "I take 30 minutes to read newspaper".

- "Peter takes a break (5 minutes) before he reviews his class notes (40~50 minutes)".

- "Tom goes to school either by train (10~30 minutes); or by bus (at least 20 minutes)".

The TPN representations of these three examples are given in Figs. 2(a), (b) and (c), respectively. For simplicity and without lost information, sometimes we represent a temporal proposition or event by a transition, see Fig. 2(d).

It is noted that the third example includes disjunctive relation.

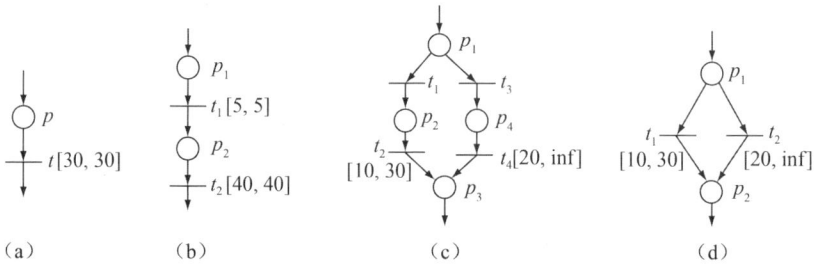

Fig. 2 TPN representation of Dechter's metric information. (a) p, t: "I read newspaper 30 minutes"; (b) p_1, t_1: "Peter takes a break (5 minutes)", p_2, t_2: "Peter reviews his class notes (40~50 minutes)"; (c) p_2, t_2: "Tom goes to school by train (10~30 minutes)"; p_4, t_4: "Tom goes to school by bus at least 20 minutes"; (d) Simplified representation of (c): t_1: "Tom goes to school by train (10~30 minutes)"; t_2: "Tom goes to school by bus at least 20 minutes"

B. Allen's Interval Relations

Given any two intervals, there are thirteen distinct ways which they can be related.[1] These temporal qualitative relations indicated how the two intervals relate in time whether they overlap, meet, precede, etc. Using the representation of [1], these relations are indicated graphically by a timeline representation of Fig. 3(a). We only show seven of the thirteen relations since the remainder are inverse relations (for example, after is the inverse relation of before). For inverse relations, given any two intervals relation, it is possible to represent their relation by using the non-inverse relations only exchanging the interval labels (the equality relation has no inverse).

Let X and Y be propositions with temporal intervals t_x and t_y, respectively. Let t_{z_1} and t_{z_2} be transitions with interval $[1, \infty)$[①]. We construct a TPN for each relation, given in Fig. 3(b). We present following theorem relating temporal intervals to TPN:

Theorem 1: Given any two propositions specified by Allen's temporal intervals, there exists a TPN representation for their temporal relation.

Proof: Let the interval t_x and t_y be $[x_s, x_e]$ and $[y_s, y_e]$ respectively, see Fig. 4. The relation "X during Y" means that the event X occurs after the event Y and the event X ends before the event Y. We want to prove the TPN representation of the temporal relation in Fig. 4(b) satisfies: $y_s < x_s < x_e < y_e$. There are only two firable transitions t_{z_1} and t_y after the transition t_1 fires. The relation $y_s < x_s$ holds because there exists a non-zero delay t_{z_1} before the transition t_x can fire. It is trivial that the relation $x_s < x_e$ holds. For the upper (branch) firing sequence in the Fig. 4(b), there exists a non-zero delay t_{z_2} after the t_x fires before reaches t_2, which means

---

① For simplicity and without restriction of generality, here we assume that the time unit is 1 and the minimum start time is 1. One could always use any finite positive rational number instead of 1.

that the transition t_x finishes firing before the token arrives at the place p_7 (t_y finishes firing). So the relation $x_e < y_e$ holds. Therefore we have $y_s < x_s < x_e < y_e$. Using the similar way, we can easily prove that each of Fig. 3(b) is the TPN representation of corresponding Allen's temporal interval relation in the Fig. 3(a). It is easily to represent the remainder six inverse relations of Allen's possible thirteen relations by using the non-inverse relations only exchanging the interval labels. We have reached the conclusion.

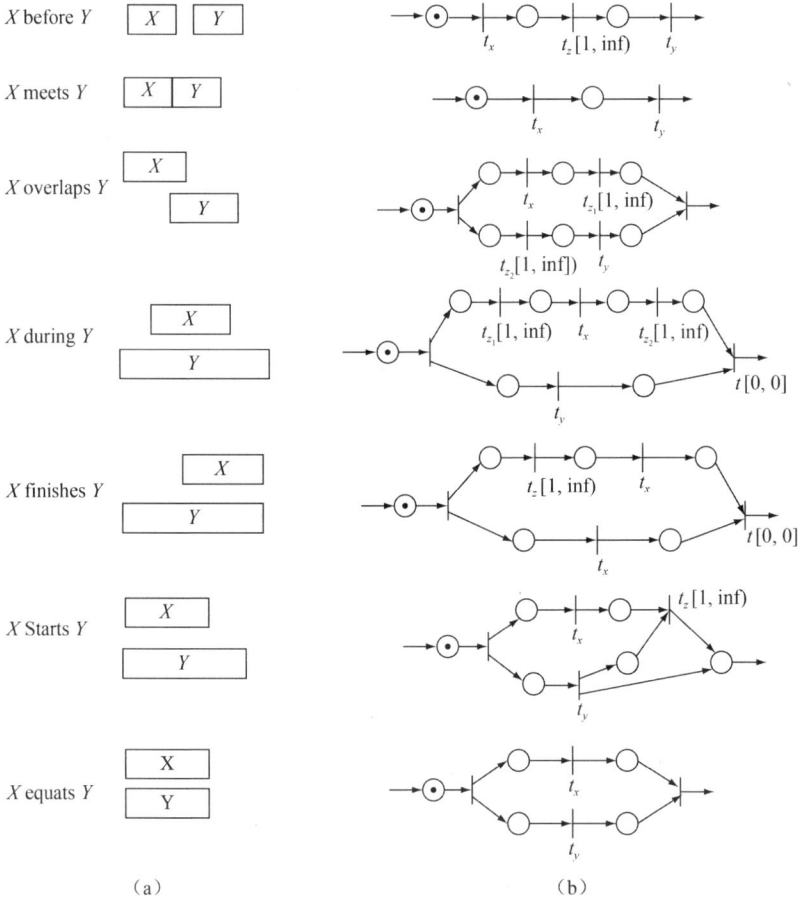

(a)　　　　　　　　　　　　　　　　(b)

Fig. 3　(a) Interval relations; (b) Corresponding TPN

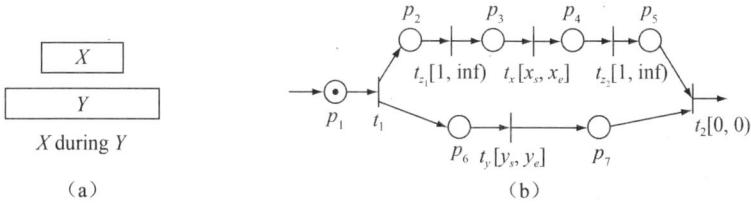

Fig. 4 Illustration of the Theorem 1's proof: (a) Allen's interval relation: "X during Y"; (b) Corresponding TPN

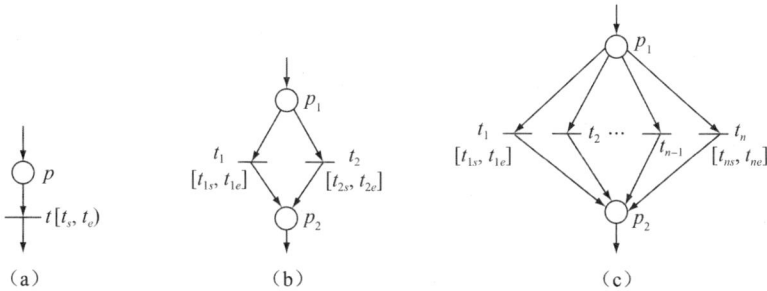

Fig. 5 Illustration of the Theorem 2's proof: TPN representation of Dechter's metric constraints

From previous subsection, any proposition specified by Dechter's metric constraint can be naturally represented by a TPN, combining with theorem 1, we give the following theorem relating metric and interval temporal constraints to TPN:

Theorem 2: For any proposition(s) specified by Dechter's metric constraints and Allen's temporal intervals, there exists a TPN representation for their temporal constraints.

Proof: It is a straightforward to prove that there exists a TPN representation for Dechter's metric constraints. Firstly, if t_s and t_e are two time points, a Dechter's metric constraint on their temporal points could be of the form $t_e - t_s \leqslant c$ where c is a positive real number. The constraint can be easily represented by a transition t

associated with firing interval $[t_s, t_e]$. By the definition of firing rule in a TPN (see section 4), the event (transition) t must fire at some moment between temporal points t_s and t_e (i. e. it cannot fire before time $t_s + \tau$ and must fire before or at time $t_e + \tau$ where τ is a time point at which the transition t is enabled). That is, the t_s and t_e in Fig. 5(a) satisfies: $t_e - t_s \leqslant c$. Secondly, to finish TPN representation of Dechter's metric constraint, we must allow disjunctive propositions. Suppose we have the following general case consisting of two disjunctive propositions $t_1 [t_{1s}, t_{1e}]$ and $t_2 [t_{2s}, t_{2e}]$: "temporal event t_1 or t_2". The TPN of the case is given in Fig. 5(b). The transitions t_1 and t_2 are disjunctive because only one of them can fire

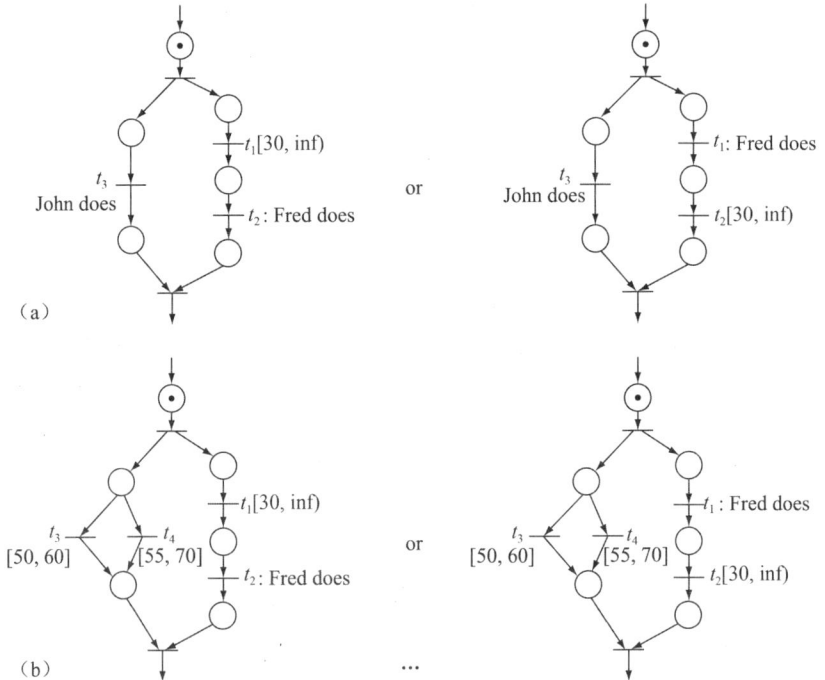

(a)

(b)

Fig. 6 (a) TPN representation of higher-order expression ("John drives to work at least 30 minutes more than Fred works"); (b) TPN representation of higher-order expression: another example with more information. t_2: "Fred drives to work"; t_3: "John goes to work by his new car"; t_4: "John goes to work by his old car"

once the place p_1 holds a token (i.e., both t_1 and t_2 are firable). The TPN of multiple disjunctive propositions t_1, t_2, $\cdots$, t_n is given in Fig. 5(c).

Therefore, for any proposition(s) specified by Dechter's metric constraints, there exists a corresponding TPN representation. Combining with above result and theorem 1, we have proved theorem 2.

C. Higher-Order Expression and Repeated Activities

In this subsection, we use two examples to illustrate how a TPN model represents the higher-order expression and repeated activities.

One of works which are still needed to extend in [6] is to explore the representation of higher-order expressions, for example, "John drives to work at least 30 minutes more than Fred does". The TPN model of this example is given in Fig. 6 (a). Furthermore, the example could be extended to "John goes to work either by his new car (50~60 minutes), or by his old car (55~70 minutes), John drive to work at least 30 minutes more than Fred does". The TPN model of this extended example is shown in Fig. 6(b).

There are a lot of repeated activities in our daily life, for example, "Tom has breakfast ($20 \sim 30$ minutes) before reads the newspaper ($30 \sim 35$ minutes) everyday. The TPN representing this kind of information is given in Fig. 7.

D. An Example

We give the TPN representation, based on discussion of previous sections, of an example with more temporal constraints.

Example 1 Tom leaves home at $7:00$ (t_1). Tom goes to school

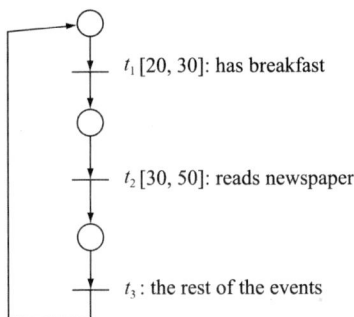

Fig. 7　TPN representation of repeated activities

either by train (t_2) (10 ~ 30 minutes), or by bus (t_3) at least 20 minutes. Once he arrives at the school, he either has breakfast (t_5) (30 ~ 40 minutes) and reads the newspaper (t_8) during his breakfast and then goes to the classroom or plays tennis with Peter (t_{12}) (20 ~ 40 minutes) and then they drink cola (t_{13}) (10 ~ 15 minutes). They go to the classroom after drinking. Peter leaves home 7:10-7:20 (t_{10}). He walks to school (t_{11}) (10~15 minutes). Once he arrives at school, he either plays tennis with Tom (t_{12}) (20~40 minutes) and then they drink cola (t_{13}) (10~15 minutes), or he reviews his class note (t_{15}) (5~10 minutes) after takes a break (5 minutes) and then goes to the classroom. [①]

The TPN representation of the example is given in Fig. 8. The dot line may represent the repeated activities if Tom and Peter perform at their daily life. This example contains metric temporal constraints but also interval relations and repeated activities.

Note that there is no deadlock in the TPN of Fig. 8 because the transition t_{12} doesn't fire though it is firable at some point. It is

---

① The transitions which do not mention here are auxiliary.

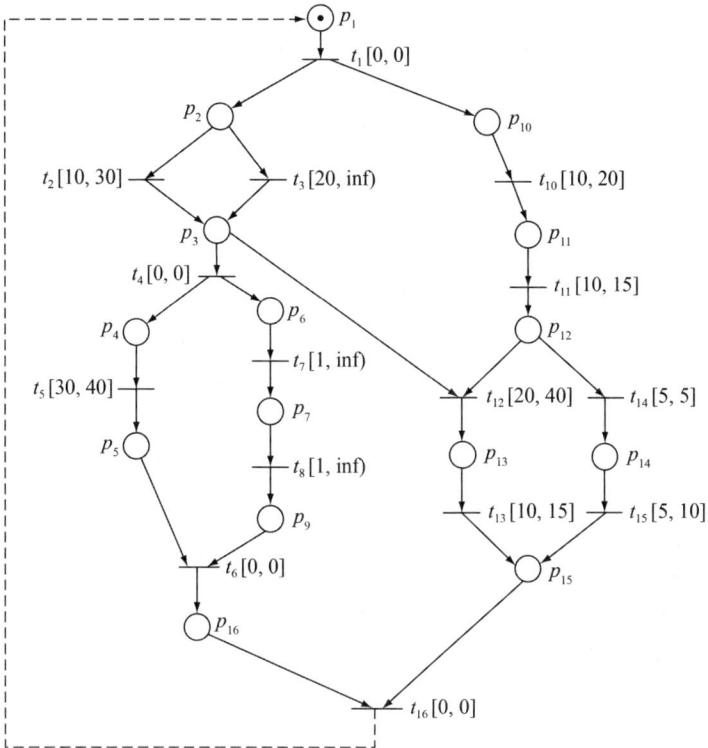

Fig. 8　TPN representation of example 1

possible that there exists a deadlock in an ordinary Petri net, but there doesn't exist any deadlock in a corresponding TPN by associating a temporal constraint with each transition of the ordinary net. The reason is that the temporal constraints in a TPN have changed the behavior of the net. The examples can be found in [25].

4. TPN ESG and Reasoning

We have constructed a TPN model for representing temporal constraints. In this section we will introduce the firing rules and extended state graph (based on [2, 15]) and then relate them to temporal reasoning.

The example 1 includes both metric and qualitative temporal constraints. Given temporal information of this kind, we want to derive answers to query such as "Is the information represented consistent?"; "Is it possible that proposition P holds at some time?". If yes, "What's event sequence with temporal information to reach P?", and "Is it possible that both temporal propositions P and Q hold at some time?".

Let us formally give the firing rule and the concept of extended state graph of a TPN before we answer these questions.

The Extended States (over states in an ordinary Petri net) in a TPN will be pairs $ES = (M, I)$ consisting of a marking M and a firing interval set I which is a vector of possible firing times. The number of entities in this vector is given by the number of the transitions enabled by marking M. These firing intervals for the enabled transitions may be different from their static firing intervals, they will be simply referred to as dynamic firing intervals and their lower and upper bounds as (dynamic) EFTs and (dynamic) LFTs, respectively.

A transition t_i is firable from $ES = (M, I)$ at time $\tau + \theta$ iff both the following conditions hold:

(1) t_i is enabled marking M at time τ:

$$(\forall p)(M(p) \geqslant B(t_i, p))$$

as in ordinary Petri nets;

(2) the relative time θ, relative to the absolute enabling time τ, is not smaller the EFT of transition t_i and not greater than the smallest

of the LFT's of all the transitions enabled by marking M:

$$\text{EFT of } t_i \leqslant \theta \leqslant \min \{\text{LFT of } t_k\}$$

where k ranges over the set of transitions enabled by M.

Note that condition 2 holds because, at time $\theta = \min \{\text{LFT of } t_k\}$ the corresponding transition, the one for which the LFT is minimum, must fire, modifying the marking and so the state of the TPN. Delay θ is not a global time; it can be seen as given by a virtual clock, local to the transition, that must have the same timing unit (e. g., in terms of seconds) than the others in the TPN. Then, as θ is relative to the time τ at which state ES has been reached, the absolute firing time, at which t_i may be fired, is defined when needed as "$\theta +$ the absolute time τ at which state ES has been reached".

Firing an enabled transition t_i, at a time θ, from this state ES leads to a new state $ES' = (M', I')$ computed as follows:

(1) The new marking M' is computed, for all places p, as

$$(\forall p)M'(p) = M(p) - B(t_i, p) + F(t_i, p),$$

as usually in Petri nets;

(2) The new firing intervals I' for transitions are computed as follows:

i) For all transitions not enabled by M', then empty;

ii) For all transition t_k enabled by marking M and not in conflict with transition t_i, i. e., transitions which remain enabled, then

$$I' = (\max (0, \text{EFT } k - \theta_{max}), \text{LFT } k - \theta_{min})$$

where EFT k and LFT k denote the lower and upper bound of interval in I corresponding to t_k, respectively.

iii) All other transitions have their firing interval set equal to their static firing interval.

In other words, the transitions not enabled by the new marking M' receive empty intervals. The transitions enabled by M and not in conflict with t_i have their intervals shifted by the value θ towards the time origin and truncated to one nonnegative value. The remaining transitions (those enabled by M' and either in conflict with t_i or not enabled by M) have their interval set to their static firing interval.

The firing rule permits one to compute states and a reachability relation among them. The set of states that are reachable from the initial state or the set of firing schedules feasible from the initial state. We define this set as follows:

*Definition 2: An Extended State Graph (**ESG**) is a tree of states. Its root is the initial **ES** and there is an arc labeled with t_i from state **ES** (node) to state **ES**' (node) if t_i is firable from **ES** and if its firing leads to state **ES**'.*

In an *ESG,* each state has only a finite number of successors, at most one for each transition enabled by the marking of the state. The *ESG* characterizes the behavior of the TPN and the possible temporal constraints of propositions which the TPN represents.

In order to illustrate a firing, let us consider the following example:

Example 2 Johnson leaves home at 7:00 am (t_1). He goes to school either by train (t_2) (15~20 minutes), or by bus (t_3) (at least 25 minutes. Once he arrives at school, he either has breakfast (t_4) (30~40 minutes) and then arrives at the classroom (t_9), or plays chess with Eric (t_5) (100~120 minutes) and then discusses/evaluates the result (t_6) (15~25 minutes) after playing. Eric also leaves home at 7:00 am (t_1). He walks to school (t_7) (5~10 minutes). Once he arrives at school, he either reads the newspaper (t_8) (40 minutes) and then arrives at the classroom or plays chess with Johnson (t_5) (100~200 minutes) and then discusses/evaluates the result (t_6) (15~25 minutes) after playing. They arrive at the classroom after discussion (t_9).

In this example, we want to query "Is the given information consistent?" i "Is it possible Johnson and Eric play chess and then discuss?" i "Is it possible that Johnson has breakfast and Eric reads the newspaper at some time?". If yes, "What's event sequence can reach this situation"? If Johnson goes to school by bus, is it still possible (i.e. "Johnson has breakfast and Eric reads newspaper at some time")? The TPN representation of example 2 is shown in Fig. 9.

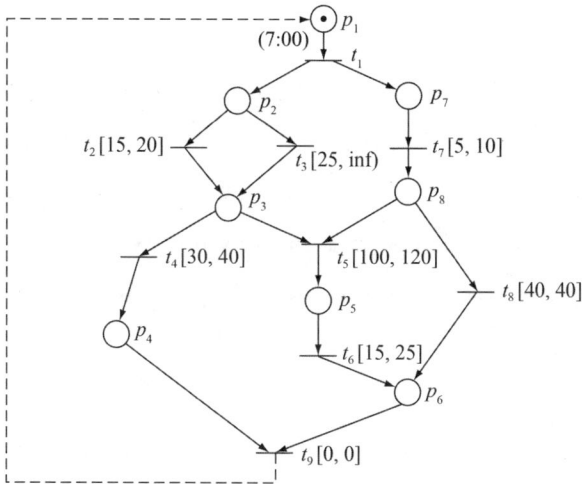

Fig. 9   TPN representation of example 2

Let us consider the TPN of Fig. 9. Obviously, $ES_1 = (M_1, I_1)$, where $M_1 = (p_1)$ and $I_1 = (t_1[0, 0])$. I_1 has only one entry, because t_1 is the only transition enabled by M_1. Firing t_1, at time $\theta = 0$, leads to the $ES_2 = (M_2, I_2)$ with $M_2 = (p_2, p_7)$ and $I_2 = (t_2[15, 20], t_3[25, \infty), t_7[5, 10])$ having three entries because transitions t_2, t_3 and t_7 enabled by M_2. Firing t_7 is allowed between the relative time value 5, the minimum value of $[5, 10]$, and the relative time value 10, the minimum value of the maximum values, in this case the minimum value of 20 for t_2, ∞ for t_3, and 10 for t_7. Firing t_7, at time θ, for any value in a potentially infinite number of values in $[5, 10]$, for instance 6, leads to next state ES_3. Finally, we can get the ESG of the net as shown in Fig. 10.

In order to relate the property of a TPN to our model, we define:

Definition 3: *A representation R is **consistent** if each proposition in R holds at some time. The R is **inconsistent** if at least one of proposition in R cannot hold at any time.*

In our TPN model, each proposition corresponds to a transition, so the proposition holds at some time t iff the corresponding transition is firable at time t. As stated above, an ESG consists of all possible states in which a TPN can reach and the possible transitions between them. Based on this observation we have the following theorem:

Theorem 3: *The representation R is consistent iff all transitions in its corresponding TPN are firable.*

Let us consider the ESG in Fig. 10. We find that the transitions t_5 and t_6 are not firable at any time, so we conclude that the R is not consistent. Whether a transition is firable corresponds to whether its corresponding proposition holds, so we can conclude that it is

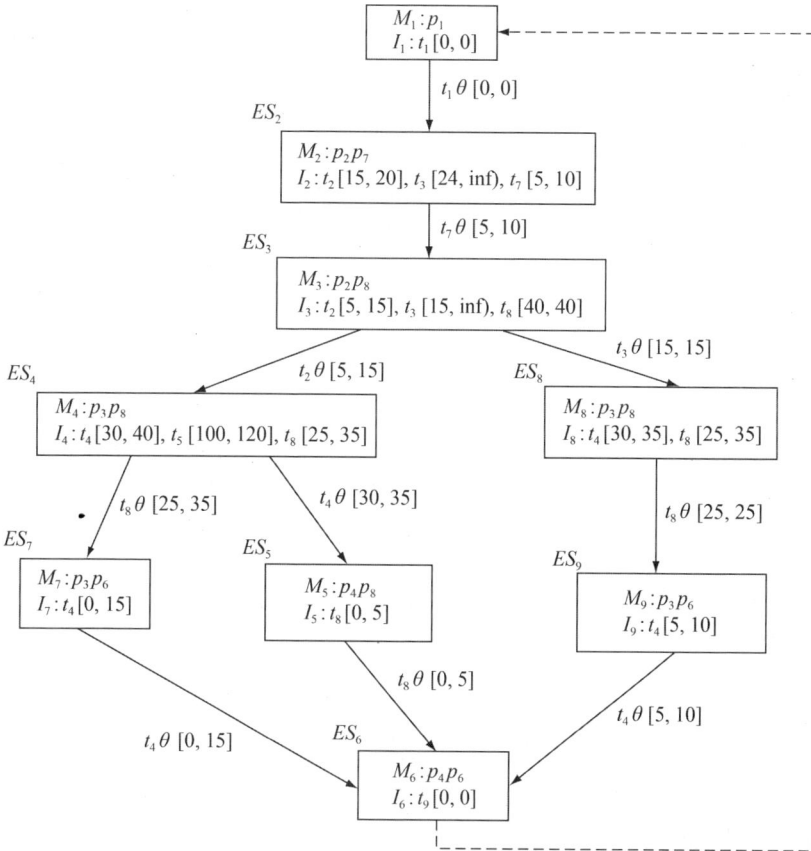

Fig. 10　The ESG of the Fig. 9

impossible that Johnson plays chess with Eric and then discuss. We also know that it is possible that Johnson reads the newspaper at some time because in Fig. 10, t_4 is firable at state ES_4.

Let the transitions t_i and t_j correspond to the propositions P_i and P_j, based on the definition of firing and ESG, we have:

Theorem 4 : *There exist some temporal relationship between P_i and P_j iff both t_i and t_j at same state ES_k are firable.*

Again, let us consider the ESG in Fig. 10, we find that both t_4

and t_8 are firable under same state ES_4. Thus we can conclude that it is possible that Johnson has breakfast and Eric reads newspaper at some time. Also, we find that there exists only one event sequence to reach this situation (ES_4): $t_1 t_7 t_2$, which means to reach this situation, Johnson has to take train. Thus we can conclude that it is impossible that the situation occurs if Johnson goes to school by bus. The more propositions and details on the relationship between the ESG and temporal constraints can be found in [25].

Also, we can use the existed software packages as mentioned at the end of Section 2 to get the results based on the firing rule and state definition given above.

5. Conclusion and Future Work

We have presented a unified TPN model for representing temporal information including metric, qualitative interval, higher-order expression and repeated activities. We relate the ESG to temporal relations and get some results through the example.

Knowledge representation and reasoning for temporal information are of considerable fundamental interest in artificial intelligence (AI) area and the TPN method has not been addressed in AI literature. As the approach for analyzing a TPN using an ESG tool can produce large sets of states, even when the size of knowledge base is small, our further works will concentrate on developing efficient algorithm to analyze the model.

Furthermore, it is interesting to relate some other concepts and properties of Petri nets to our model. Two of structural properties of

Petri nets, repetitiveness (a Petri net with the incidence matrix A is [partially] repetitive iff there exists a vector x of positive [nonnegative] integers such that $A^Tx \geq 0$, $x \neq 0$.) and fairness[17], can be directly applied to determine whether or not some temporal events occur infinitely often in a sequence. This is particularly important for the repeated activities. In Petri nets theory, invariants are important properties of the logical structure of a Petri net, and therefore characterize in some way all possible firing behaviors. Invariants associated with places are usually called S-invariants (formally, y is a S-invariant if y is an integer solution of $Ay = 0$ where A is the incidence matrix) and represent unchanging truths about sets of conditions, such as disjunctive situations in our model. Invariants associated with transitions are usually called T-invariants (formally, x is a T invariant if x is an integer solution of $A^Tx = 0$ where A is the incidence matrix) and represent collections of transitions that, when fired, leave the marking of the Petri net unchanged; therefore, like the repetitiveness and fairness, T-invariants are important for studying repetition. The concept of synchronic distance (proposed by Petri in 1976) represents a well-defined metric for some subclasses (marked graph and C/E system) of general Petri nets. [10] One may probably use the properties of the synchronic distance to improve the result of the Theorem 4 and give more accurate temporal relationship. However, there are some difficulties when it is applied to more general class of Petri nets. [18]

Acknowledgment

The author would like to thank the following people: Peter Allen for his generous support when the author was with the Columbia University; Minglun Fang and Bole Shi for their encouragement while the author initiated the work; Diana Litman for her helpful comments on earlier drafts of this paper; Ying Chen, David C. Yao, RongXian Ma, Juhong He and Shihua Yao for their continued support in the course of this study; and finally to anonymous referees for their constructive comments on the paper.

References

[1] James F. Allen, "Maintaining Knowledge about Temporal Intervals", *Communications of ACM* Vol. 26, No. 11, pp. 832-843, 1983.

[2] Bernard Berthomieu and Michel Diaz, "Modelling and Verification of Time Dependent Systems Using Time Petri Nets", *IEEE Trans. on Software Engineering* Vol. 17, No. 3, pp. 259-273, 1991.

[3] Shyi-Ming Chen, Jyh-Sheng Ke and Jin-Fu Chang, "Knowledge Representation Using Fuzzy Petri Nets", *IEEE Trans. on Knowledge and Data Engineering* Vol. 2, No. 3, pp. 311-319, Sept. 1990.

[4] Rene David and Hassane Alla, *Petri Nets and Grafcet*, Prentice-Hall Press, 1992.

[5] Rina Dechter, Itay Meiri and Judea Pearl, "Temporal Constraint Network", in *Proceedings of the First International Conference on Principles of Knowledge Representation and Reasoning*, San Mateo, CA, 1989, Morgan Kaufmann Publishers, Inc..

[6] Rina Dechter, Itay Meiri and Judea Pearl, "Temporal Constraint Network", *Artificial Intelligence* Vol. 49, pp. 61-95, 1991.

[7] Yi Deng and Shi-Kuo Chang, "A G-net Model for Knowledge Representation and Reasoning", *IEEE Trans. on Knowledge and Data Engineering* Vol. 2, No. 3, pp. 295-310, Sept. 1990.

[8] F. Frunet et al., "Prototyping Discrete Systems Control for Faster Debugging and Implementation", in *Proceedings of 16th Annual Conference of IEEE Industrial Electronics Society*, pp. 694-699, California, 1990.

[9] Paul Freedman, "Time, Petri Nets, and Robotics", *IEEE Trans. on Robotics and Automation* Vol. 7, No. 4, pp. 417-433, 1991.

[10] G. Goltz and Chong-Yi Yuan, "Synchronic Structure-a Tutorial", in G. Rozenberg, ed., *Advances in Petri Nets, Lecture Notes in Computer Sciences* Vol. 222, Springer Verlag, New York, 1986.

[11] Henry Kautz and Peter Ladkin, "Integrating Metric and Qualitative Temporal Reasoning", in *Proceedings of AAAI-91*, pp. 241-246, Anaheim, CA, 1991.

[12] Massimo Kautz and Ronald Brachman, "Metric Constraints for Maintaining Appointments: Dates and Repeated Activities", in *Proceedings of AAAI-91*, pp. 253-259, Anaheim, CA, 1991.

[13] J. Malik and T. Binford, "Reasoning in Time and Space", in *Proceedings of 8th IJCAI*, pp. 343-345, Karlsruhe, FRG, 1983.

[14] Itay Meiri, "Combining Qualitative and Quantitative Constraints in Temporal Reasoning", in *Proceedings of AAAI-91*, pp. 260 - 267, Anaheim, CA, 1991.

[15] Miguel Menasche and Bernard Berthomieu, "Time Petri Nets for Analyzing and Verifying Time Dependent Communication Protocols", in *Proceedings of 3rd International Workshop on Protocol Specification, Testing and Verification*, Ruschlikon, Switzerland, 1983, Amsterdam, The Netherlands: North-Holland.

[16] P. Merlin and D. Farbor, "Recoverability of Communication Protocols", *IEEE Trans. on Communications* Vol. 24, No. 9, pp. 1036-1043, 1976.

[17] Tadao Murata, "Petri Nets: Properties, Analysis and Applications", *Proceedings of IEEE* Vol. 77, No. 4, pp. 541-580, 1989.

[18] Tadao Murata and Z. Wu, "Fair Relation and Modified Synchronic Distance in a Petri Nets", *Journal of Franklin Institute* Vol. 320, No. 2, pp. 63-82, Aug. 1985.

[19] J. L. Peterson, *Petri Net Theory and Modeling of Systems*, Englewood Cliffs, NJ: Prentice-Hall Inc., 1981.

[20] C. V. Ramamoorthy, "Performance Evaluation of Asynchronous Concurrent Systems Using Petri Nets", *IEEE Trans. on Software Engineering* Vol. 6, No. 5, pp. 440-449, 1980.

[21] W. Resig, *Petri Nets*, Springer Verlag, New York, 1991.

[22] Grzegorz Rozenberg, "Advances in Petri Nets", *Lecture Notes in Computer Science* Vol. 524, Springer Verlag, New York, 1991.

[23] R. Valette, "Nets in Production Systems", in W. Braver et al. eds., *Petri Nets-Applications and Relationships to Other Models of Concurrency, Lecture Notes in Computer Sciences*, Vol. 255, Springer Verlag, New York, 1987.

[24] Marc Vilian, Henry Kautz and Peter van Beek, "Constraint Propagation Algorithms for Temporal Reasoning: A Revised Report", in Hohan deKleer

and Dan Weld eds., *Readings in Qualitative Reasoning about Physical Systems*, Morgan Kaufmann Publishers, Inc., 1989.

[25] Yulin. Yao, *Temporal Reasoning Using an Extended State Graph* (in preparation).

[26] Yulin Yao, *Uncertain Temporal Information Representation Using Petri Nets* (in preparation).

[27] Yulin Yao, "An Approach to Formal Specification and Analysis for Time Performance of the Concurrent Real Time System", *International Journal of Computer in Industry* (Elsevier Science Publishers B. V), Vol. 12, No. 4, pp. 347-354, 1989.

[28] Yulin Yao, "Petri Net: An Approach of Modelling for Information System", *Nature Journal* Vol. 12, No. 12, pp. 883-889, 1989.

[29] Yulin Yao, "The Specification of a Snoopy Cache-coherence Protocol Based on Petri Nets", in *Second ORSA Conference on Telecommunications*, Boca Raton, FL, 1992.

[30] Yulin Yao and Zhenfei Sun, "Simulating the Communication in the Distributed System", in *Proceedings of Beijing International Conference on System Simulation and Scientific Computing*, pp. 199-204, Beijing, October 1989. CSSC, IMACS and SCS-International.

6

Computing Robust Viewpoints with Multi-constraints Using Tree Annealing[①]

1. Introduction

Sensor planning involves determining strategies with which sensor parameter values can be found that will achieve a sensing task with a certain degree of satisfaction. It is a fairly new area of computer vision but has received considerable interest recently.[2, 6-8] Tarabanis, Tsai and Allen[7] have been developing a vision planning system, Machine Vision Planner (MVP), that automatically determines vision sensor parameter values so that the task requirements are satisfied. Compared to the iterative techniques employed in the SRI system[2] and other sensor planning systems, the main contribution of the MVP system is that it provides closed-form solutions to the individual task constraints and determines a set of sensor parameters which characterize the general viewing configurations. However, in the MVP system, it is

① Final draft. Co-author: Peter Allen. *Proceeding of IEEE International Conference on Systems, Man and Cybernetics – Intelligent Systems for the 21st Century*, Vancouver, Canada, Oct. 22-25, 1995, pp. 993-998.

difficult to compute robust viewpoints which satisfy all feature detectability constraints simultaneously. As Tarabanis pointed out in [6], techniques that combine the admissible domain of individual constraints to determine optimal solutions still need to be investigated.

In this paper, the viewpoint setting is formulated as an unconstrainted optimization problem, then a tree annealing (TA) technique[1] which is one of simulated annealing algorithms[4] that can handle continuously valued variables, is applied to solve the multiple nonlinear constraints problem. Our results show that the technique is quite effective to get robust viewpoints even in the presence of considerable amounts of noise.

2. Constraints for Feature Detectability

In the MVP system, the configurations of viewing parameters that are planned include the three positional degrees of freedom of the sensor $r_a(x, y, z)$, the two orientational degree of freedom (pan and tilt angles) described by a unit vector v along the viewing direction and the three optical parameters (the back nodal point to image plane distance d, and focal length f and the aperture of the lens a). Thus, planning is done in eight-dimensional space and a point in this space is defined as a generalized viewpoint $V(r_o, v, d, f, a)$. Using knowledge from geometry and optics, each task constraint in the MVP is characterized by an analytical relationship.[6] As a result, the locus of generalized viewpoints that satisfies the resolution, depth-of-field and field-of-view constraints separately is expressed by a relationship of the form: $g_i(r_o, v, d, f, a) \geq 0$, specifically:

- Depth of field:

  for farthest point: $g_1 = D_1 - \| (r_o - r_f) \cdot v \| \geq 0$,

  for closest point: $g_2 = \| (r_o - r_c) \cdot v \| - D_2 \geq 0$,

where r_f is the position vector of the farthest feature vertex from the front nodal point of the lens along the viewing direction; r_c is the position vector of the closest feature vertex from the front nodal point of the lens along the viewing direction; r_o is the position vector of the front nodal point of the lens and

$$D_1 = \frac{Daf}{af - c(D - f)}, \quad D_2 = \frac{Daf}{af + c(D - f)}, \quad D = \frac{1}{(1/f - 1/d)},$$

where c is the minimum of the horizontal and vertical sensor element spacings, d is the back nodal point to image plane distance, f is the focal length and a is the aperture of the lens.

- Field of view:

$$g_3 = (r_k - r_o) \cdot v - \cos\left(\frac{\alpha}{2}\right) \| r_k - r_o \| \geq 0,$$

where $r_k = r_c - R_o v$, r_c is the position vector of the center of the sphere of radius R_f circumscribing the object features, $R_o = R_f/[\sin(\alpha/2)]$, R_f is the radius of the sphere circumscribing all the object features, α is the field of view angle and is given by $\alpha = 2 \cdot \tan^{-1}(I_{min}/2d)$, I_{min} is the minimum dimension of the sensor plane, and all other variables are as defined above.

- Resolution for edge feature $\overline{AB}_i$:

$$g_4 = \frac{\| v \times [e_i \times (r_o - r_{A_i})] \|}{[(r_{A_i} - r_o) \cdot v][(r_{B_i} - r_o) \cdot v]} - \frac{w}{dl} \geq 0,$$

where r_o, r_{A_i}, r_{B_i} are the position vectors of the front nodal point of the lens and vertices of the feature edge i to be resolved; e_i is the unit vector along to feature edge $\overline{AB_i}$ to be resolved; l, w are the lengths of the feature to be resolved in object and image space, respectively. All other variables are as defined above.

Unit vector:

$$g_5 = \| v \|^2 - 1 = 0.$$

It should be noted that there is a resolution constraint for each edge feature that is to be resolved, while for other constraints, there is a single relationship for all features.

3. Tree Annealing

Tree annealing[1, 3] is an extension of the familiar Metropolis algorithm[5] of simulated annealing but handles continuously valued variables in a natural way. In this section, we briefly introduce the tree annealing (TA) method based on [1, 3].

Following the definitions and notations of [1, 3], let us assume we are searching for the minimum of some function $f(x)$ where the d-dimensional vector x has continuously valued elements. Furthermore, we assume a finite search space $S \subset R^d$. A k-d tree in which each level of the tree represents a binary partition of one particular degree of freedom (DOF) is used. Each node may thus be interpreted as representing a hyperrectangle, and its children therefore represent the smaller hyperrectangles resulting from dividing the parent along one particular DOF.

Let a vector x be the current sample. At each node, two numbers are stored, n_L and n_R, representing how many times in the past that an acceptable point has been found in the left and right subtrees, respectively. The TA algorithm works as follows for a finite set S:

(1) Growing and searching the tree:

a. The tree is initiated by simply creating the rootnode, and choosing a point at random with uniform probability from the entire search space. That point becomes the first accepted point. Two daughter nodes are created, corresponding to a division of the search space in half along the first DOF. The n_L and n_R are both initialized to 1 for the root node.

b. Begin at the root and, at each node, choose either the left or right child randomly with probability $\dfrac{n_L}{n_L + n_R}$ or $\dfrac{n_R}{n_L + n_R}$ respectively. Descend the tree to its leaves making left-right decisions in this way.

c. Upon reaching a leaf, generate the point y at random (uniformly) from the subspace defined by the leaf. Compare x and y and make an accept/reject decision on x (see step 2). If y is accepted, replace x by y as the current sample; if y is rejected, x remains the current sample.

d. If y was accepted, split the current leaf (containing y), and create two new daughter nodes, thus making more resolution available at this node if it is ever explored again.

e. Ascend the tree from the current sample to the root, updating n_L and n_R at each node.

(2) Accept/reject decision. Accept the point y as the new

estimate with probability

$$\min \left(1, \frac{g(x)}{g(y)} \frac{p(y)}{p(x)}\right),$$

where the probabilities p are Gibbs, $\Big($ i. e., with form $p(\lambda) \propto$ $\exp\left(-\frac{f(x)}{T}\right)\Big)$ and $g(y)$ is computed from the path of the descent down the tree by

$$g(y) = \frac{1}{V_y} \prod_l p_l',$$

where $p_l' = \frac{a_l}{a_l + b_l}$, l represents the node visited at level l, a_l represents n_L or n_R, according to which direction was chosen ar each l. Similarly, b_l represents the n of the direction not chosen.

(3) The annealing schedule is very similar to the suggestion in [4]:

$$T \leftarrow rT,$$

where $r = 1 - \frac{dS}{C_v}$ and dS is a small positive constant and C_v is a term easily related to the variance of the energy.

4. Problem Formulation

The decisive criteria of a computed viewpoint are its robustness and stability. The measure is used to assess the goodness of a solution with respect to the value of each constraint relationship g_i. This is appropriate since a large positive value of g_i indicates that a constraint is satisfied comfortably, a small positive value indicates marginal satisfaction, while inadmissible solutions give rise to a negative value. We want to search a globally admissible eight-dimensional viewpoint which is near the center of the admissible domain and far from the bounded hypersurfaces described by the constraints. Such a generalized viewpoint is desirable, since it is robust in the event of inaccuracy. Similarly, the measure for the visibility constraint is also formulated. For this purpose, the minimum distance, d_v, from the viewpoint to the polyhedron describing the visibility region is chosen: $g_6 = \pm d_v$, where $+ d_v$ or $- d_v$ depending on whether the point is inside or outside the visibility volume respectively. The optimization function is taken to be a weighted sum of the above component criteria, each of which characterize the quality of the solution with respect to each associated requirement separately. If we take two edge features then we will have two resolution constraints g_{4a} and g_{4b}, each of them with respect to an edge feature. Thus, the optimization function is written as:

$$\max_S obj = \sum_i \alpha_i \cdot g_i (i = 1, 2, 3, 4a, 4b, 6),$$

$$\text{or } \min_S obj = - \sum_i \alpha_i \cdot g_i (i = 1, 2, 3, 4a, 4b, 6).$$

Subject to:

$$g_i \geqslant 0; \ i = 1, 2, 3, 4a, 4b, 6; \text{ and } g_5 = 0,$$

where α_i are weights and s is a point of the finite eight-dimensional space S.

We convert the above set of constraints into a penalty function. For each $g_i (i = 1, 2, 3, 4a, 4b, 6)$, the penalty term $\exp (- \beta_i g_i)$ is assigned, where β_i is a positive real number which represents the degree of penalty (penalty factor). It is appropriate since, for $g_i < 0$, the value of the exp ($-\beta_i g_i$) will be (exponentially) very large; for $g_i \geqslant 0$, the value of the exp ($-\beta_i g_i$) will be small. For g_5, the penalty term exp ($\beta_5 |g_5|$) is assigned, where β_5 is a positive penalty factor. In our experiments, we choose same penalty factor ($= 1$) for each constraint $g_i (i = 1, 2, 3, 4a, 4b)$. It is also appropriate since, for $g_5 = 0$, exp ($\beta_5 |g_5|$) $= 1$; for $g_5 \neq 0$, the value of exp ($\beta_5 |g_5|$) will be (exponentially) very large. In our experiments, we choose $\beta_5 = 1\,000$, which is larger than any other penalty factor, in order to get more accurate unit vector. So we know that the penalty function will appropriately penalize any infeasible/inadmissible constraint. Thus the constrained problem is reformulated as an unconstrainted optimization:

$$\min_{s \in S} obj = - \sum_i \alpha_i \cdot g_i + \sum_i \exp(-\beta_i \cdot g_i) + \exp(\beta_5 \cdot |g_5|)$$

where $i = 1, 2, 3, 4a, 4b, 6$.

We use the TA algorithms described in the previous section to solve this unconstrainted optimization.

5. Experimental Results

As part of the MVP system, we have implemented the vision planning algorithms that are given in section 2 and 3 using the TA algorithm. In the experiments, we will demonstrate the effectiveness of applying the technique to compute the robust general viewpoints with multiple feature detectability constraints. The features to be observed are the two edges (a and b) of an enclosed cube.

In our experiments, we choose the parameters as in [6]: $r_C =$

$(0, 0, 0)$, which coincides with the origin of object coordinates system; $c = 13.5$ microns, $l = 2.54$ mm, $w = 0.021\ 12$ mm, $I_{min} = 6.5$ mm, where c is the minimum of the horizontal and vertical sensor element spacings, l, w and I_{min} are defined in Section 2. The values of the lens aperture a and the intrinsic focal length f are chosen a priori ($f = 12.5$mm and $a = f/16 = 0.781\ 25$ mm) and thus, values for the remaining imaging space parameters v and d are computed. All measured units are expressed in millimeters in the experiments. The values of the weights α_i in the objective function are taken to be: $\alpha_1 = 0.1$, $\alpha_2 = \alpha_3 = 0.01$, $\alpha_{4a} = \alpha_{4b} = 1\ 000$. The values of the weights β_i in the penalty function are taken to be: $\beta_1 = \beta_2 = \beta_3 = \beta_{4a} = \beta_{4b} = \beta_6 = 1$, $\beta_5 = 1\ 000$ (explained in previous section).

An initial viewpoint V_i that is chosen to start the optimization, and the corresponding camera viewpoint V_f that is computed by the TA algorithm, is listed in Tab. 1 . For V_i, the g_1 and g_3 constraints are violated (refer to the first column in the Tab. 2). All feature detectability of constraints of the computed viewpoint V_f that is determined by the TA algorithm are satisfied.

Tab. 1 The initial and final generalized viewpoints V_i and V_f (unit: mm)

	x	y	z	$v(1)$	$v(2)$	$v(3)$	f	d	a
V_i	80.0	-5.0	160.0	-0.58	0.2	-0.8	12.5	14.0	$f/16$
V_f	124.34	-4.44	207.60	-0.61	-0.03	-0.79	12.5	13.13	$f/16$

In order to check the robustness and stability of the computed viewpoints, the camera is approached to the object along the view direction to see whether the constraints are still satisfied. Let P_1 be the computed viewpoint, P_2 be a point at which the camera approaches the object and C be the center of the sphere of circumscribing the object features. The approaching scale factor is defined as follows:

$$\text{scale factor} = \frac{|\overrightarrow{P_1 P_2}|}{\text{the projection of } \overrightarrow{P_1 C} \text{ on the view direction } \overrightarrow{P_1 P_2}}.$$

We find all constraints but g_2 and g_3 are satisfied. The constraint g_2 (depth of field for closest point) is isolated when the distance between the viewpoint and the center of the object is less than the certain value (D_2); and the constrain g_3 (focus of view) is isolated when the angle between the view direction $\overrightarrow{P_1 P_2}$ and $\overrightarrow{P_2 C}$ is greater than certain value. These values are determined by the intrinsic parameters of camera (see the definition of g_2 and g_3 in section 2). The interesting result of the maximum reachable viewpoint $V_{\max}$, which still satisfy simultaneously all constraints, from the current computed viewpoint V_f respectively along a reverse view direction, is given in the third column in Tab. 2.

Another factor that will affect the stability and robustness of the computed viewpoint is the presence of noise, for example, the slight perturbation of manipulator on which the camera is mounted (we can imagine that the manipulator is teleoperated and many conditions around it are unpredictable). In order to check the stability and robustness of viewpoint planning in the presence of noise, independent random noise with 10%, 20% and 30% are added to each component of the position vector r_o and the orientation vector v. The values of constraints under the different noise levels are listed in Tab. 2. We can find from the table that all constraints are still satisfied in these cases, that is, the computed viewpoint V_f are stable and robust even in the presence of noise. Thus, we can conclude that the viewpoint V_f which is computed by the TA algorithm is robust and stable.

Tab. 2 The values of constraints with the different scale factors and noises for V_i,

V_f and V_{max} (unit: mm)

	V_i	V_f	V_{max}	scale factor			noise		
				0.10	0.25	0.50	0.10	0.20	0.30
x	80.00	124.34	215.23	109.63	87.57	50.80	135.57	140.48	134.73
y	−5.0	−4.44	−9.62	−3.60	−2.35	−0.25	−4.45	−5.17	−4.91
z	160.00	207.60	324.96	188.61	160.13	112.66	219.39	209.41	225.02
$v(1)$	−0.58	−0.61	−0.61	−0.61	−0.61	−0.61	−0.65	−0.69	−0.67
$v(2)$	0.20	0.03	0.03	0.03	0.03	0.03	0.04	0.04	0.04
$v(3)$	−0.80	−0.79	−0.79	−0.79	−0.79	−0.79	−0.82	−0.87	−0.93
f	12.50	12.50	12.5	12.50	12.50	12.50	12.50	12.50	12.50
d	14.00	13.13	13.13	13.13	13.13	13.13	13.13	13.13	13.13
a	f/16	f/16	f/16	f/16	f/16	f/16	f/16	f/16	f/16
g_1	−42.98	150.36	1.83	174.39	210.44	270.52	134.73	139.54	128.62
g_2	52.09	28.75	177.28	4.71	−31.33	−91.42	44.58	39.74	49.99
g_3	−8.53	1.55	7.22	0.34	−1.98	−11.17	2.02	3.26	3.52
g_{4a}	0.004 7	0.003 1	0.001 6	0.003 5	0.004 5	0.007 6	0.002 8	0.002 8	0.002 7
g_{4b}	0.002 1	0.001 6	0.000 8	0.001 8	0.002 2	0.003 1	0.001 5	0.001 7	0.001 4

Acknowledgments

The authors would like to thank Steven Abrams and Paul Michelman for their valuable help and comments.

References

[1] Griff Bilbro and Wesley Snyder, "Optimization of Functions with Many

Minima", *IEEE Transactions on Systems, Man and Cybernetic* 21 (4): 840-849, 1991.

[2] C. K. Cowan and A. Bergman, "Determining the Camera and Light Source Location for a Visual Task", in *Proceedings of IEEE International Conference on Robotics and Automation*, 509-514, 1989.

[3] Younsik Han, Griff Bilbro, and Wesley Snyder, "Pose Determination Using Tree Annealing", in *Proceedings of IEEE International Conference on Robotics and Automation*, Cincinnati, OH, 1990.

[4] S. Kirkpatrick, C. Gelatt, and M. Vecchi, "Optimization by Simulated Annealing", *Science* 220 (4598): 671-680, 1983.

[5] N. Metropolis, A. Rosenbluth, M. Rosenbluth, A. Teller, and E. Teller, "Equation of State Calculations by Fast Computing Machines", *Journal of Chemical Physics* 21 (6): 1087-1091, 1953.

[6] K. Tarabanis, "Automatic Synthesis of Camera Views that Satisfy Feature Detectability Constraints", PhD thesis, Computer Science Department, Columbia University, New York, NY, 1991.

[7] K. Tarabanis, R. Y. Tsai, and P. Allen, "Automated Sensor Planning for Robotic Vision Tasks", in *Proceedings of IEEE International Conference on Robotics and Automation*, 1991.

[8] S. Yi, R. M. Haralick, and L. G. Shapiro, "Automatic Sensor and Light Source Positioning for Machine Vision", in *Proceedings of IEEE International Conference on Pattern Recognition*, 55-59, 1990.

Postscript

This paper is a part of the research I conducted as a PhD student at Columbia University. It focuses on an area of computer vision called Sensor Planning. My supervisor and senior PhD students developed a vision planning system, MVP whose main contribution is to provide an explicit solution for each task constraint and determine a set of sensor parameters. However, it is difficult for this system to compute a robust viewpoint that satisfy all the feature constraints at the same time. This paper focuses on transforming this problem into an unconstrained nonlinear optimization problem, and then applying tree annealing techniques to solve the problem computationally. The results show that this technique is quite effective in obtaining robust viewpoints even in the presence of a large amount of noise.

I would like to dedicate this paper to my advisor Professor Allen, who provided me with the opportunity to study and research at Columbia University. My only regret is that I did not stay there long enough to develop further.

7

Toward Parallel Financial Computation: Valuation of Mortgage-Backed Securities[①]

1. Introduction

The valuations of complex financial instruments in volatile interest rate environments are a vital part of risk management and asset management. Because these valuations are computationally intensive, major financial institutions such as Merrill Lynch, Citicorp and Prudential Securities have turned to highly advanced supercomputers such as Cray XMP from Cray and Paragon from Intel in search of better performance. [7] The search has largely ignored a significant pool of computational power that is already widely available in these financial institutions—large networks of relatively low-cost workstations (e. g.: Sun SPARCs, HPs, IBM RS6000s, etc.). The resources, such as processors, memory and disk space of the workstations, are lightly loaded or even idle for large periods of time.

① Final draft. Co-authors: John Cheng, Philip Enny and Duanyang Guo. *Proceeding of IEEE International Conference on Systems, Man and Cybernetics - Intelligent Systems for the 21st Century*, Vancouver, Canada, Oct 22-25, 1995, pp. 1176-1181.

As of the end of 1991, mortgages comprised 32% of the U. S. bond market outstanding, compared to only 29% in U. S. Treasury and agency securities and 17% corporate bonds. [6] In recent years, the supply of new mortgage securities has been more than twice the supply of new corporate bonds issued. At the end of 1994, the total notional value of Mortgage-Backed Securities (MBSs) and their derivatives are about $ 2. 4 trillion. In fact, only about one-third of total residential mortgages have been securitized. [10] Such observations demonstrate the importance of understanding the risks, returns and valuation of MBS.

This paper presents an MBS valuation parallel system which consists of a pool of general-purpose workstations using a message-passing mechanism. The experimental system is running in an environment consisting of up to 16 workstations. The processing time under a parallel processing scheme is significantly reduced.

2. Mortgage-Backed Securities And Cmos

Mortgage originators sell mortgages they own to buyers, or conduits. Conduits take a collection of similarly structured of mortgages and create an aggregate, or pool. As specified by the conduit upon creation, each pool has a: coupon–gross interest rate of return; pass-through rate–the rate of return passed on to the investor; issue date–the issue date of the pool; maturity date–the date the last mortgage in the collateral pool will mature; average life–average time to receipt of principal repayment. [5]

The coupon and average life are expressed as weighted averages of the underlying mortgages due to the fact that there may be non-homogeneous distribution of coupon and maturity of the underlying mortgages.

As mortgage payments are received by the conduit, pro-rated principal and interest shares of the pool, less servicing and other fees, are passed to the investor. The first such type of investment instrument, a Mortgage Pass-Through Security, was issued under the guaranty of the Government National Mortgage Association (GNMA) in 1970. Pass-throughs are the predominant form of MBS in the secondary mortgage market today. [5]

Yield-to-maturity valuations, as used for valuating government or corporate bonds, are not valid for pass-throughs due to the potentially non-homogeneous distribution of underlying pools are used. Yield-to-WAM valuations still do not provide accurate valuation of pools due to the implied call option of mortgages. The remaining principal balance, paid when the mortgage is called, increases the cash flow to the pool investor also decreasing potential future interest income from the pool investment. Prone to uncertain cash flows in volatile interest rate markets, pools provide unpredictable rates of return to investors.

In 1983, to provide protection from the implied call Mortgage Corporation (FHLMC) introduced Collateralized Mortgage Obligations (CMOs). [1, 5] CMO's, collateralized by an MBS, provided limited protection from market fluctuation by allowing investors to purchase CMO component bonds, or tranches, with defined maturities and cash flows that are protected from the implied call option of the pass-through MBS. Other tranches of the CMO absorb the inherent instability of the collateral by being the recipient of excess cash flows due to principal prepayment.

Cash flow distribution to individual tranches is defined in the CMO prospectus when the CMO is issued. Tranches that do not receive interest or principal payments until the prior tranche is retired are referred to as accrual or Z tranches. Z tranches compound any deferred interest. Planned Amortization Class (PAC) tranches have defined maturities and cash flows within a predetermined prepayment rate range. Targeted Amortization Class (TAC) tranches do not provide protection to maturity extension if prepayment rates decline. Variable interest rate tranches, or floaters, have rates that vary based upon a spread to a predetermined market index. Residual tranches receive excess principal payments due to accelerated prepayment. The valuation of CMOs is affected by market conditions such as prevailing interest rate fluctuation.

3. MBSs Option-Adjusted Analysis

The valuation and risk management of MBSs and CMOs are more complicated than those of most other fixed-income securities, because mortgages give the borrower (home-owner) the option to prepay the loan at par at any time during the life of the loan. While our understanding of risks, returns and valuations of securities with options has been derived by the seminal work of Black and Scholes[3] and the literature that has built upon that work, mortgages are much more complicated option-like securities than those dealt with by Black and Scholes (an excellent introduction can be found in [9]).

Black and Scholes assume that ① interest rates are constant; ② the option is "European" in that it could only be exercised on the final maturity date; ③ the exercise price is known and fixed; ④ the returns on the underlying asset are normally distributed. However, the volatility of interest rates is the reason that the prepayment option in a mortgage has value and is of interest. Furthermore, it may well be optimal for different people to exercise their prepayment options at different times, particularly as they have different effective costs of exercising their options. Finally, the underlying asset for the prepayment option is a bond, which does not have normally distributed returns. [1, 2, 4]

There are two methodologies commonly used to value MBSs: static cash flow yield (SCFY) and option-adjusted spread (OAS). [1, 2] The SCFY is the yield that will make the present value of the cash flows, given some prepayment assumptions, equal to the market price of the MBS. An effective duration and convexity can also be computed. The drawback of this framework is the difficulty of selecting an appropriate benchmark Treasury security.

The OAS methodology may be applied to MBSs, in which case the cash flow on the generated paths is based on a prepayment model. This methodology can be used to determine the option-adjusted spread and option cost of MBSs.

In this paper we implement a message-passing parallel OAS valuation system for mortgage securities. An OAS model is constructed upon the following building blocks: [2, 11]

• *An interest rate term structure model* is used to generate a series of future interest rate paths.

• *A prepayment model* is used to forecast the change in pool cash flow according to the interest rate paths generated and the specific collateral characteristics selected.

- *A cash flow model* is used to calculate the monthly distributions of cash flows according to the projections of the prepayment model and CMO-specific information.

The functional blocks are given in Fig. 1.

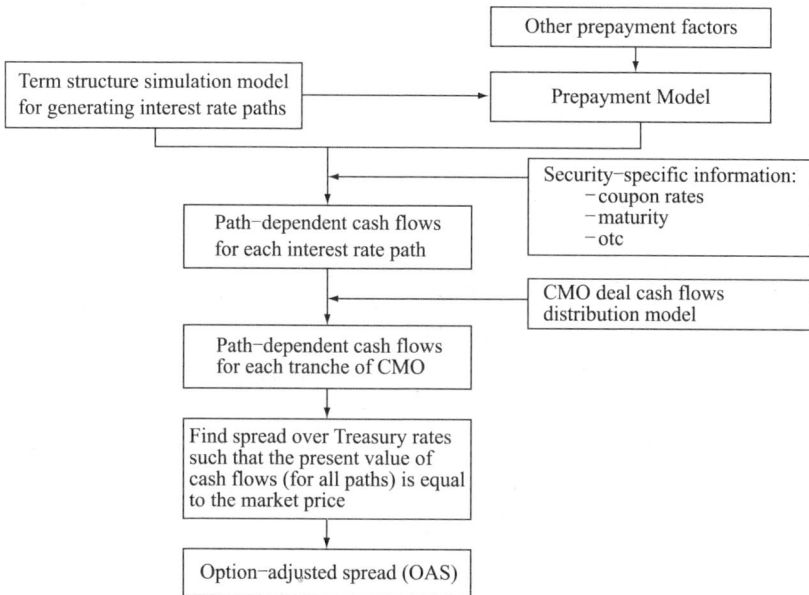

Fig. 1   Mortgage-Backed Securities Option-Adjusted Analysis

For an interest rate path ω, let r_0^ω, r_1^ω, $\cdots$ be the values of short rate on the path. For a security of maturity T periods, let CF_1^ω, CF_2^ω, $\cdots$, CF_T^ω be the cash flows, given the particular realization of interest rates. For a specified spread s, the present value of the cash flows given interest rate path ω is defined to be

$$PV^\omega = \sum_{t=1}^{T} \frac{CF_t^\omega}{\prod_{\tau=0}^{t-1}(1 + r_\tau^\omega + s)}.$$

If s is a fair spread over Treasury rates for the security, the theoretical value of the security, PV, is assumed to be the average present value over all possible interest rate paths. If K is the number of interest rate paths sampled, we estimate PV by

$$PV = \frac{1}{K} \sum_{\omega=1}^{K} PV^{\omega}.$$

The OAS for a security is the value of an s that makes PV equal to the current market price of the security. That is, the OAS is the solution of [8]

$$PV = P_{\text{market}} = \frac{1}{K} \sum_{\omega=1}^{K} \sum_{t=1}^{T} \frac{CF_t^{\omega}}{\prod_{\tau=0}^{t-1} (1 + r_\tau^{\omega} + s)}.$$

4. Parallel Implementation and Experimental Results

Assume that there are M workstations as slaves and one as a master. There are totally N paths to be computed. These paths will be distributed to M workstations and processed in parallel.

The master dispatches the paths to the slaves in batch-by-batch. In each batch, it decides how many paths and to which slaves the paths are sent for processing. The number of paths dispatched to each individual slave should be in accordance to its workload, and ideally the workloads should be balanced at all slaves. Because the workload at each slave can fluctuate over time, a dynamic load-balancing scheme should be introduced.

At the beginning of our algorithm, the master allots an equal number of paths to be dispatched to each slave. In each batch, when a slave has processed half of the paths, the average time used for computing one path at this slave is calculated and reported back to the master. The master, upon receiving feedback from all slaves, updates the allotment of paths inversely proportionate to the average time of computing a path at a slave. If a slave currently takes a longer time to process a path, it will receive a smaller number of paths in the next batch.

The specific algorithm we use is as follows:

- Initialization: $t = 0$ and let each $N_i(t)(1 \leqslant i \leqslant M)$ be N_0, where $N_i(t)$ is the number of paths to be dispatched and processed to slave i at time t.

Speed-Ups

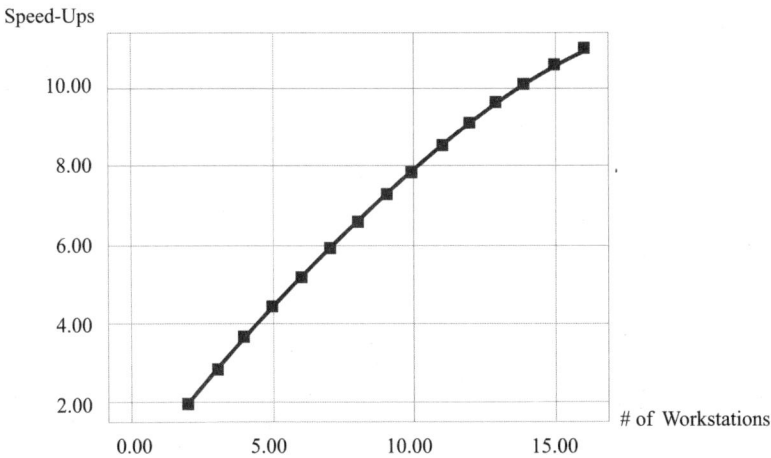

Fig. 2 The Speed-Up vs. the Number of Workstations

- Master:

i. Step 1: dispatches $N_i(t)$ paths to slave i for $i = 1, 2, \cdots, M$ and then waits to receive a response from all slaves. The message from slave i $(1 \leqslant i \leqslant M)$ represents the time for computing a path at slave i, $T_i(t)$.

ii. Step 2: upon receiving the messages from all stations, it updates $N_i(t+1)$ with $\dfrac{N_i(t)\sum_{i=1}^{M}T_i(t)}{M\cdot T_i(t)}$.

iii. Step 3: $t \leftarrow t+1$ and go back to Step 1.

- Slave i $(1\leqslant i\leqslant M)$:

i. Step 1: when half of paths in this batch are processed, it calculates the average time used for a path, $T_i(t)$, and reports to the master.

ii. Step 2: upon having processed the rest of paths in batch t, $t \leftarrow t+1$ and go back to Step 1.

We have conducted the experiment in an environment consisting of up to 16 Hewlett-Packard workstations($M=16$). The speed-ups under different configurations are computed (shown in Fig. 2). Clearly, the performance (measured by speed-up) scales up as the number of workstations used increases-when 16 workstations are used, the performance nicely scales to 11 times the single system performance.

Tab. 1　The Relative Processing Time, Speed-Ups vs. the Number of Workstations Used

(here we assume the processing time for one workstation = 100.0)

# of Workstations	1	2	4	6	8	10	12	14	16
Relative Processing Time	100.0	52.4	27.5	19.2	15.1	12.7	11.1	10.0	9.1
Speed-Up		1.9	3.6	5.2	6.6	7.9	9.0	10.1	11.0

5. Conclusion

We implemented an MBS valuation parallel system which consists of a cluster of general purpose workstations using a message-passing mechanism. The experimental system is running in an environment consisting of up to 16 workstations. The processing time under parallel processing scheme (16 workstations) is significantly reduced. the performance (measured by speed-up) scales up as the number of workstations used increases. When 16 workstations are used, the performance nicely scales to 11 times the single system performance.

The framework presented in this paper is open to different interest rate models and prepayment models. Theoretically speaking, the number of workstations in the system is unlimited (however, more workstations could imply higher communications cost). Furthermore, to explore maximum possible resources utilization ratio in an international firm, we can easily extend our system to a wide-area network (WAN) linked by a dedicated line or Internet, so that a system in the New York office may use lightly loaded computers in the Tokyo office during off peak hours and vice versa.

To achieve an optimal dynamic load-balancing strategy, one need carefully choose the parameters in the algorithm. These parameters include N_0 and the number of paths in a batch at time t which slave i needs to report back to master.

Acknowledgments

First author would like to thank Shree Nayar for his generous support. Authors also wish to thank the following people: Norman Desharnais and Larry Landau for helpful comments and suggestions; Paul Descloux, Joseph Gallgher and Juemin Sun for their reading on earlier draft of this paper.

References

[1] William W. Bartlett, " *Mortgage-Backed Securities: Products, Analysis, Trading*", New York Institute of Finance, 1988.

[2] William W. Bartlett, " *The Valuation of Mortgage-Backed Securities*", Richard D. Irwin, Inc., 1994.

[3] Fischer Black and Myron S. Scholes, "The Pricing of Options and Corporate Liabilities", *Journal of Political Economy* 637-659, May/June 1973.

[4] Douglas Breeden, "Risk, Return and Hedging of Fixed-rate Mortgages", *Journal of Fixed Income* 85-98, September 1992.

[5] Frank J. Fabozzi eds., *The Handbook of Mortgage-Backed Securities (3E)*, Probus Pub. Co., 1992.

[6] Frank J. Fabozzi, *Bond Markets, Analysis and Strategies*, Prentice-Hall Inc., 1993.

[7] Tom Groenfeldt, "Choose your Weapons", *Risk Technology Supplement* August 1994.

[8] Lakhbir S. Hayre and Kenneth Lauterbach, "*Stochastic Valuation of Debt Securities*", Prudential-Bache Financial Strategies Group, 1988.

[9] John Hull, " *Option, Futures and Other Derivatives Securities (2E)*", Prentice-Hall Inc., 1993.

[10] Inside Mortgage Securities (an MBS industry newsletter), January 1995.

[11] Stephen D. Smith, "Analyzing Risk and Return for Mortgage-backed Securities", in *Financial Derivatives: New Instruments and Their Uses*, Federal Reserve Bank of Atlanta, December 1993.

Postscript

Collateralized Mortgage Obligations (CMOs), derivatives of Mortgage-Backed Securities (MBS), are complex and at the same time important financial derivatives with demanding pricing calculations. In the early 1990s, it took minutes or tens of minutes to price a CMO. This was unacceptable in the rapidly changing financial markets. Wall Street firms at the time typically used mainframe computers such as IBM 370 or even supercomputers such as Cray, but the results were not particularly favorable. This prompted us to explore the computation of CMOs, the main means of which was to parallelize the computation of CMOs in a distributed fashion for fast computing.

I would like to dedicate this article to Linda Becker of Dow Jones Telerate, who brought me into the financial industry from a layman with zero knowledge of finance and no knowledge of mortgages; and my good friend and colleague Phil. It is because of their support and encouragement that I was able to enter a whole new industry that I am still enjoying 30 years later.

8

A Trinomial Dividend Valuation Model[①]

The dividend discount model (DDM), the most widely used method of common stock valuation, equates the stock price to the discounted value of its expected future dividends. Financial text such as Bodie, Kane and Marcus [1995] traditionally recommend estimating the dividend series by applying a constant growth rate to the current dividend (the Gordon growth model) or by partitioning the expected dividend series into several parts with different growth rates. These models have become standard tools for equity research groups operating in leading brokerage houses, commercial banks, money management firms and institutional investment setting (Rappaport [1986]).

Although widely used, the Gordon model is criticized for its assumptions, especially the assumption that growth is both geometric and indefinite. Hurley and Johnson [1994] present a realistic dividend valuation model (HJ model) that improves on the Gordon model by:

• introducing an additive model, which estimates the value of

① Final draft for submission with some comments from a reviewer. *Journal of Portfolio Management* Vol. 23, No. 4, 1997: 99-103.

the firm where the dividend payment changes (increases or remains constant) a fixed amount.

- assuming that, in each period, the firm will either keep its dividend same or increases it, in contrast to the Gordon model, where the dividend growth rate is a constant number.

Hurley and Johnson illustrate their model by computing the values of three telephone utilities. Two of the three firms keep the dividend constant for some periods. Their models give more accurate estimate than the Gordon's.

In the real world, it is not uncommon for a firm to reduces dividends temporarily. Let's take the electric utilities industry as an example. The common dividend payment index of the industry decreased three times in past 15 years (see the Value Line Industry Review [1995]). To get a better estimate of the value for such firms, it is necessary to incorporate the possibility that these firms will reduce their dividend.

Hence, in this paper, we extend the HJ to take reduced dividend payments into account for both the additive and geometric cases. We assume that, in each period, a firm will either increase its dividend with a probability p^u, decrease its dividend with a probability p^d or keep it constant with p^c. Based on this assumption, we derive a simple closed-form solution to estimate the value of the firm. We show that the HJ model (the Gordon model) is a special case of our model when $p^d = 0$ (when $p^d = p^c = 0$).

We use our model, termed a Trinomial Dividend Valuation Model (TriDVM), to compute the value of five selected electric utilities firms that temporarily reduced dividend payments at some point in last fifteen years. The results show that our model, in general, produces better price estimates than the HJ model.

Trinomial Dividend Valuation Model（TriDVM）

As in Hurley and Johnson's [1994] approach, we assume that, in each period, a firm will either increase its dividend with a probability p^u, decrease its dividend with a probability p^d or keep it constant with p^c. Let D_t be the dividend at period t. Given this assumption, we know that D_t ($t \geqslant 0$) is a Markov chain since the dividend D_{t+1} at time $t+1$ only depends on dividend D_t at time t and is independent of $D_s(s < t)$.

TRIDVM: Additive Model

Let D_t be the dividend at period t. The dividend D_t either increases by an amount Δ with probability p^u, decreases by same amount with probability p^d, or stays the same with probability $p^c = 1 - p^u - p^d$:

$$D_{t+1} = \begin{cases} D_t + \Delta & \text{with probability } p^u, \\ D_t - \Delta & \text{with probability } p^d, \ t = 0, 1, 2, \cdots, \\ D_t & \text{with probability } p^c = 1 - p^u - p^d. \end{cases}$$

If the dividend increases in period 1, the stockholder will receive the dividend $D_0 + \Delta$ and the value of the stock $V_A(D_0 + \Delta)$. If the dividend decreases in period 1, the stockholder will receive the dividend $D_0 - \Delta$ and the value of the stock $V_A(D_0 - \Delta)$. If the dividend stays the same in period 1, the stockholder will receive the dividend D_0 and the value of the stock $V_A D_0$.

Let k be the return an investor must earn to hold the stock. The price of the stock or present value is equal to the expected value of cash flows:

$$V_A(D_0) = p^u \frac{D_t + \Delta + V_A(D_0 + \Delta)}{1 + k} + p^d \frac{D_t - \Delta + V_A(D_0 - \Delta)}{1 + k}$$
$$+ p^c \frac{D_t + V_A(D_0)}{1 + k}.$$

Solving this equation, we have following additive mode (see the endnotes for more details on how to solve the equation):

$$V_A(D_0) = \frac{D_0}{k} + \left[\frac{1}{k} + \frac{1}{k^2}\right](p^u - p^d)\Delta. \tag{1}$$

Note that, when $p^d = 0$, the model becomes the HJ model.

TriDVM: Geometric Model

The dividend D_t either increases by a constant percentage amount g with probability p^u, decreases by same amount with probability p^d, or stays the same with probability $p^c = 1 - p^u - p^d$:

$$D_{t+1} = \begin{cases} D_t(1 + g) & \text{with probability } p^u, \\ D_t(1 - g) & \text{with probability } p^d, \quad t = 0, 1, 2, \cdots, \\ D_t & \text{with probability } p^c = 1 - p^u - p^d. \end{cases}$$

Using the same reasoning as in the addition model, we have the geometric model (see Endnote 2 for an interesting comment from a reviewer as to how to expand this model):

$$V_G = \frac{1 + (p^u - p^d)g}{k - (p^u - p^d)g} D_0. \tag{2}$$

Note that when $p^d = 0$, the model becomes the HJ model; when $p^d = p^c = 0$, the model becomes the Gordon model.

TriDVM: Lower Bounds

If we assume that, for each period, there is a probability p^b that the firm will go bankrupt, for an additive process, we have:

$$V_A(D_0) = \begin{cases} \dfrac{D_0 + \Delta + V_A(D_0 + \Delta)}{1 + k} & \text{with probability } p^u, \\[3mm] \dfrac{D_0 - \Delta + V_A(D_0 - \Delta)}{1 + k} & \text{with probability } p^d, \\[3mm] \dfrac{D_0 + V_A(D_0)}{1 + k} & \text{with probability } p^c = 1 - p^u - p^d - p^b, \\[3mm] 0 & \text{with probability } p^b. \end{cases}$$

Solving this equation using a similar method given in the previous section, we get a closed form estimate L_A under the additive Markov process, which gives a lower bound of the estimate:

$$L_A = \frac{1 - p^b}{k + p^b} D_0 + \left[\frac{1}{k + p^b} + \frac{1 - p^b}{(k + p^b)^2} \right] (p^u - p^d)\Delta. \qquad (3)$$

Similarly, we can calculate a lower bound L_G for a geometric process:

$$L_G = \frac{1 - p^b + (p^u - p^d)g}{k + p^b - (p^u - p^d)g} d_0. \qquad (4)$$

Exhibit 1 gives the lower bounds for both additive and geometric models, L_A and L_G for various values of k and p^b, given $D_0 = 2.5$, $\Delta = 0.25$, $p^u = 0.80$, and $p^d = 0.10$.

Exhibit 1   Tridvm with Possibility of Bankruptcy:

L_A for Various Values of k and p^b

	L_A for Various p^b			L_G for Various p^b		
k	0.01	0.02	0.03	0.01	0.02	0.03
0.10	38.41	33.78	30.04	34.17	29.85	26.45
0.12	30.64	27.50	24.88	26.97	24.17	21.85
0.14	25.37	23.11	21.17	22.28	20.30	18.61
0.16	21.58	19.88	18.39	18.98	17.50	16.21
0.18	18.75	17.41	16.23	16.53	15.38	14.36
0.20	16.55	15.48	14.51	14.64	13.72	12.88

$D_0 = 2.5$, $p^u = 0.80$, $p^d = 0.10$, $\Delta = 0.25$ for the additive model, and $g = 0.05$ for the geometric model.

PRACTICAL EXAMPLES

To test our models, we select five electric utilities that have had regular dividend payments in the past fifteen years. All firms selected also have had experiences of temporarily reducing their dividend payments for some periods. The five companies are Rochester Gas & Electric, United Illuminating, Ohio Edison, Montana Power, and Sierra Pacific Resources. Exhibit 2 gives historical dividend data for the past fifteen years for these firms. All data are taken from Value Line Investment Survey [1995].

Exhibit 2   Dividend History of Selected Electric Utilities Firms

	Rochester		Ohio	Montana	Sierra
Year	G & E	UI	Edison	Power	Pacific
1979	1.33	2.62	1.76	1.03	1.28
1980	1.40	2.68	1.76	1.06	1.43

（续表）

	Rochester		Ohio	Montana	Sierra
Year	G & E	UI	Edison	Power	Pacific
1981	1.49	2.76	1.76	1.17	1.46
1982	1.75	2.92	1.76	1.27	1.46
1983	1.84	3.08	1.80	1.46	1.50
1984	2.04	2.30	1.84	1.30	1.57
1985	2.20	2.08	1.88	1.00	1.63
1986	2.20	2.32	1.92	1.26	1.69
1987	2.03	2.32	1.96	1.34	1.74
1988	1.50	2.32	1.96	1.35	1.77
1989	1.52	2.32	1.96	1.39	1.81
1990	1.58	2.32	1.73	1.44	1.84
1991	1.62	2.44	1.50	1.50	1.84
1992	1.68	2.56	1.50	1.55	1.48
1993	1.72	2.66	1.50	1.55	1.12
1994	1.76	2.76	1.50	1.59	1.12
Beta	0.60	0.60	0.75	0.75	0.60

We first estimate the discount rate k using the capital asset pricing model (CAPM):

$$k = r_f + \beta E(r_M - r_f)$$

where the risk-free rate (T-bill yield) $r_f = 6\%$, the market risk premium $E(r_M - r_f) = 5\%$, and the betas (βs) are from value line.

For each firm, using the historical information given in Exhibit 2, we estimate the Δ and g from the past pattern of dividend changes and the probabilities p^u (p^d) from the number of years the dividend increases (decreases) over fifteen years. Finally, we compute the values V_A and V_G of the five stocks using the HJ model and our

TriDVM models (see Exhibit 3).

Exhibit 3 also gives the actual price and the best fit model. Note that, for the HJ model, we assume that the probability p in their equations is equal to p^u. This implies that both p^d and p^c will be counted into $1 \sim p$.

Exhibit 3   Tridvm Valuations of the Firms

Company	HJ model		TriDVM		Actual	Best Fit
	V_A	V_G	V_A	V_G	Price	
Rochester G & E	27.91	40.05	24.63	28.39	23.00	V_A: TriDVM
UI	40.63	46.87	36.79	39.09	35.00	V_A: TriDVM
Ohio Edison	19.74	19.82	18.73	18.74	19.00	V_G: TriDVM
Montana Power	19.68	33.02	17.40	21.91	24.00	V_G: TriDVM
Sierra Pacifc	21.88	24.60	19.58	20.27	19.00	V_A: TriDVM

It is surprising how well our models predict the actual stock prices. It is not surprising, however, that our models, in general, produce better estimates than the HJ model since the TriDVM models extend the HJ models by taking reduced dividend payments into consideration. Note that all five firms temporarily reduced their dividend payments in the past fifteen years for some periods. Of course, the TriDVM's estimate of value will be same as HJ model's for firms which have not experienced reduced dividend payments in the past.

You may notice that the additive model works better for some firms and the geometric model for others. The reason is that each firm has its own pattern of dividend payments.

For example, for Montana Power, the additive model in Equation (1) gives a price estimate of $17.40. The geometric model in Equation (2) gives a price estimate of $21.91, which is much closer to the actual price of ＄24.00 than the additive model, and is consistent with the firm's pattern of dividend payments. On the other hand, for Sierra Pacific, the additive model in Equation (1) gives a price estimate of ＄19.58. The geometric model in Equation (2) gives a price estimate of ＄20.27. Obviously, the price estimate of the additive model is closer to actual price of ＄19.00, which is consistent with the firm's pattern of dividend payments.

As stated by Hurley and Johnson, whether the analyst should choose an additive model or a geometric model depends on analyst's forecast of the pattern of dividend payments. The additive model might be the choice as the valuation model for firms with relatively erratic dividend patterns, while the geometric model might be the choice for firms with relatively stable dividend payments.

CONCLUSIONS

We derive a simple closed-form solution to estimate the value of the firm and show that the HJ model and the Gordon model are special cases of our model. We use our model to compute the values of five selected electric utilities firms that temporarily reduced their dividend payments in past fifteen years. The TriDVM model provides a new way to estimate the value of the firm in these circumstances. The results show that our model, in general, produces better price estimate than the HJ model.

ENDNOTES

The author would like to thank the following people: Marlon Balrop, Phil Enny and Helina Frydman for their helpful comments on earlier draft of this paper; Bob Litterman, Ravi Narula, Jae Sang and Jeff Weiss for their reading of the paper; and an anonymous referee for his constructive comments on the paper.

(1) We want to solve:

$$V_A(D_0) = p^u \frac{D_t + \Delta + V_A(D_0 + \Delta)}{1 + k} + p^d \frac{D_t - \Delta + V_A(D_0 - \Delta)}{1 + k}$$

$$+ p^c \frac{D_t + V_A(D_0)}{1 + k}.$$

Simplifying the equation, we have:

$$V(x) = b_0 + ax + b_1 V(x + \Delta) + b_2 V(x - \Delta),$$

where

$$a = \frac{1}{p^u + p^d + k},$$

$$b_0 = \frac{p^u - p^d}{p^u + p^d + k}\Delta,$$

$$b_1 = \frac{p^u}{p^u + p^d + k},$$

$$b_2 = \frac{p^d}{p^u + p^d + k},$$

$$x = D_0.$$

This is a linear recurrence relation with constant coefficients (see Liu [1977]). Solving this equation and letting the number of periods approach to infinity, we have following additive model:

$$V_A = \frac{D_0}{k} + \left[\frac{1}{k} + \frac{1}{k^2}\right](p^u - p^d)\Delta,$$

where V_A is the estimate of value, D_0 is the dividend payment at time 0 (current dividend), k is the return an investor must earn to hold the stock, and the firm's dividend either increases by an amount Δ with probability p^u, decreases by same amount with probability p^d or stays the same with probability $p^c = 1 - p^u - p^d$.

(2) As a reviewer pointed out, for a more generalization version of geometric model, one can derive a model with different growth rates for when the dividend goes up and when it goes down. Also, the growth rate for each period is not necessarily same. It is not trivial matter, however, to estimate growth rate for each period and growth rates for when the dividend goes down.

References

[1] Zvi Bodie, Alex Kane, and Alan J. Marcus, *Investments*, 3rd ed. Burr Ridge. IL: ichard D. Irwin, Inc., 1995.

[2] "Electric Utilities", in *Value Line Industry Review*, October 13, 1995, pp. 2-238.

[3] "Electric Utilities Industry", in *Value Line Investment Survey*, October 13, 1995.

[4] Myron J Gordon, *The Investment, Financing and Valuation of the Corporation*, Homewood, IL: Richard D. Irwin, 1962.

[5] William J. Hurley, and Lewis D. Johnson, "A Realistic Dividend Valuation Model". *Financial Analysts Journal*, July/August 1994, pp. 50-54.

[6] Chung L. Liu, *Elements of Discrete Mathematics*, New York: McGraw-Hill, Inc., 1977.

[7] Alfred Rappaport, " The Affordable Dividend Approach to Equity Valuation". *Financial Analysts Journal*, July/August 1986, pp. 52-59.

Postscript

The "Trinomial Dividend Valuation Model" presented in this paper improves on one of the most popular security valuation models in finance and tests valuation scenarios for five utility companies. The model shows better results than earlier forms of the Gordon model.

Linda Becker at Dow Jones took an extended medical leave of absence, and I decided to leave as well. I joined Goldman Sachs' Global Markets Risk Management and Asset allocation Group in New York. Goldman Sachs is well known on Wall Street for its long hours, rigor, and high quality.

While working at Goldman Sachs, I started my part-time MBA program at NYU Stern School of Business, which lasted three and a half years.

Looking back, it was probably the most intense three and a half years of my life. In addition to my daily work at Goldman Sachs, I usually attended classes at the school from 8:00 pm to 10:00 pm, worked and studied at least 100 hours a week, and slept no more than 5 hours a day on average.

In such an intensive environment, it would be easy to give up or put off part-time study. But the professors at the Stern School of Business, with their deep understanding of their fields and passion for teaching, always encouraged me to be on the pursuit for more knowledge. The professors are not only known for their world-class research, but also for their passion for teaching and caring for their students. At the time, Professor Martin Gruber was already a well-known scholar, but he still spent a lot of time with the MBA students in his classes. It was because of his encouragement that I sent this paper to the *Journal of Portfolio Management*. Because of my academic performance, I was awarded the Stern Scholar, only 1% or 2% students receiving the title, and it was even rarer among the part-time MBA students.

It was an unforgettable experience.

I would like to dedicate this article to the professors at NYU Stern School of Business, represented by professor Martin Gruber, who are not only great teachers, but also world-leading researchers in their fields. It is fascinating that a layman like me was able to learn a great deal about finance and other business aspects in just three and a half years, providing a solid foundation for my entire professional life.

I would also like to dedicate this article to my former colleagues at Goldman Sachs, Bob Litterman and Jeffrey Weiss, to name a few, whose outstanding talent, diligence, and commitment to excellence have always been a source of encouragement to me.

9

Long / Short Equity Hedge Fund Investing: Are Sector Specialists Better Than Generalists?[①]

Historically hedge funds attracted primarily high net worth individual investors. In the past several years, because of increasing market volatility, hedge funds have gained in popularity among institutional and individual investors as a way to dampen their portfolio volatility. Total assets under management (AUM) in the hedge fund industry are estimated to be between $ 650 billion and $ 700 billion and an additional $ 50~ $ 100 billion of assets are estimated to be in private managed accounts within hedge funds.[1] Among the various hedge fund strategies, the Long/short equity strategy is the largest and represents about 35. 5% of all hedge fund assets according to TASS [2003].[2]

Long/short equity funds can be divided into two groups: Long/short sector specialists ("specialists") and Long /short generalists ("generalists"). Specialists are those Long/short equity managers who exploit opportunities and invest in only one relatively narrowly defined sector of the market such as financial services, health care, or

---

① Final draft. Co-authors: Brian Clifford and Rodney Berens. *Journal of Wealth Management* Vol. 7, No. 1, Summer 2004, pp. 35-43.

technology. Generalists are Long/short managers who can invest across many or even all sectors of the market.

Conventional wisdom is in favor of the specialists for their focus, dedication, and specialty on the sector. For example, a health care investor who formerly worked as a physician might understand the dynamics of the health care industry and better determine which companies will be winners and which will be losers. Conversely, it is argued that generalists have more opportunities across various sectors.

It is important for hedge fund investors (e. g., foundations and endowments, funds of hedge funds, pension funds, and high net worth individuals) to understand the risk/return tradeoff between specialists and generalists. For investors who want to diversify their long-only portfolio by adding Long/short equity managers, it is crucial to know the difference in diversification benefits of specialists and generalists under various degrees of market dislocations.

Unfortunately, research comparing specialists and generalists has not been well documented. Several recently published studies focus on analyzing the differences between hedge fund strategies and long-only investments. Ineichen [2002] compares Long/short sector specialists to their long-only peers and concludes that Long/short managers offer higher risk-adjusted returns and lower correlation between managers. Kao [2002] examines whether alpha and return distributions from hedge funds and long-only portfolios are due to different risk factors.

The question we set out to answer is whether there is any evidence to support one approach versus the other when looking at them as a group. In this article, we use various approaches to empirically examine and compare generalists versus sector specialists by focusing on the following aspects: [3]

- Manager's ability to manage systematic risk

- Performance after adjusting for the volatility of corresponding benchmarks and percent of managers with skill in market timing

- Percent of managers with skill in each sub-group of managers after accounting for benchmark exposure and non-synchronous pricing issues

- Diversification benefits and fund performance in periods of extreme market dislocation

It is important for us to realize that generalists and sector specialist hedge funds invest in different universes or markets with different risk and return characteristics. These universes and markets can be benchmarked by different long only market indexes. One should not use a broad market index such as Russell 3 000 to measure the skill of health care specialists as the risk and return of the health care industry is different from those for the broad market. To evaluate the manager skills of the generalists and specialists relative to the market they invest, our study uses the board market index for evaluating generalists and various sector market indexes for evaluating corresponding sector specialists.

While our study did not find evidence to support either generalists or sector specialists, this lack of evidence highlights to us the significance of choosing hedge fund managers largely through a "bottom up" process whereby individual hedge fund manager quality defined by various qualitative and quantitative measures is paramount. Furthermore, the study did highlight some interesting differences between and similarities among generalists and sector funds, which can be important when constructing a portfolio of hedge funds within a larger portfolio of multiple asset classes.

1. Data and Statistics Overview

The indices for various Long/short equity strategies used in this study were obtained from HFR, which offers the longest data history currently available, among data vendors. The HFR Equity Hedge Index is used as the benchmark for the Long/short equity generalist group.[4] The HFRI Sector Indices (Technology, Financials, and Health Care/Biotech) are used as the benchmarks for the respective Long/short equity sector specialist groups.[5] They are all equal-weighted performance indices. For long only benchmarks, we use the Russell 3 000 Index for generalists, the Nasdaq Index for the technology sector, the NYSE Financials Index for the financials sector, and the AMEX Biotech/Pharmaceutical Index for the Healthcare/Biotech sector, respectively.

Exhibit 1　Risk and Return Statistics Overview: Long/Short Equity Hedge Fund Indices

(Generalists and Sector Specialists) and Their Long-Only Benchmarks

	Generalist		Sector Specialists					
			Healthcare/Biotech		Financials		Technology	
Index Used	HFRI Equity Hedge Index	Long-Only Bmark: Russell 3 000 Index	HFRI Sector: Health Care/ Biotech Index	Long-Only Bmark: AMEX Biotech Index	HFRI Sector: Financial Index	Long-Only Bmark: NYSE Financials Index	HFRI Sector: Techno-logy Index	Long-Only Bmark: Nasdaq Composite Index
Period	1/90-5/03	1/90-5/03	1/93-5/03	1/93-5/03	1/92-5/03	1/92-5/03	1/91-5/03	1/91-5/03
Number of Months	161	161	125	125	137	137	149	149

（续表）

	Generalist		Sector Specialists					
			Healthcare/Biotech		Financials		Technology	
Annualized Return	17.1%	8.7%	19.1%	18.6%	19.2%	11.9%	20.1%	15.4%
Annualized Volatility	9.3%	15.3%	24.2%	44.8%	12.2%	17.0%	20.4%	26.8%
Worst Monthly Return	-7.7%	-15.4%	-17.7%	-28.7%	-18.7%	-21.6%	-15.2%	-22.9%
Percentage of Up Months	71%	61%	58%	49%	74%	61%	60%	62%
Sharpe Ratio	1.35	0.27	0.61	0.32	1.23	0.45	0.77	0.41
Correlation*	0.72	1.00	0.86	1.00	0.80	1.00	0.89	1.00
Alpha w.r.t Benchmark	14.2%	0.0%	11.0%	0.0%	13.2%	0.0%	10.2%	0.0%
Beta w.r.t Benchmark	0.44	1.00	0.46	1.00	0.57	1.00	0.67	1.00

* Correlation is calculated with respect to its corresponding long-only benchmark.

Exhibit 1 provides a summary of risk and return statistics for the hedge fund indices and their corresponding long-only benchmarks. As one can see from the exhibit, Long/short equity generalists and specialists have higher returns than their corresponding long-only benchmarks, yet with much lower volatility. Therefore, the risk-adjusted returns of the Long/short equity managers are much higher than their long-only counterparts.

As we discussed in the previous section, in order to have a more meaningful relative comparison of the Long/short equity generalists versus Long/short equity specialists, we used different market benchmarks (as opposed to using hedge fund indices as benchmarks or a single market index; see list above) for generalists and sector specialists to calculate relative measures such as correlation, alpha, and beta. For example, we use the Russell 3 000 Index as the market benchmark when calculating the relative measures for a generalist, the NYSE Financials Index for the financials sector specialists, the Nasdaq Composite Index for the technology sector specialists and so forth.

For an individual manager's return history, we rely on our in-house database. [6] The generalist data sample is restricted to Long / short equity generalists who have at least five years of monthly returns in our database. The number of generalists in the sample is 239. The three sector specialist samples are restricted to sector Long /short specialists who have at least three years of monthly returns. [7] The number of sector specialists for Technology, Financials, and Healthcare/Biotech are 26, 21 and 54, respectively. The total number of the sector specialists is 101. Therefore, the total number of funds in our study is 340. Our results are certainly subject to survivorship bias, as the database does not include all defunct managers. [8] However, because our study mainly focuses on the comparison between Long/short generalists and sector specialists, both are subject to survivorship bias. [9]

2. Benchmark Exposures and Correlations

Volatility as a measure of risk is an absolute measure and cannot be compared between different sets of managers who invest in completely different markets. Beta, however, is a relative risk measure that depicts a manager's volatility against a benchmark. Essentially, beta quantifies a manager's systematic risk exposure or sensitivity to a specified benchmark. We calculated trailing two-year

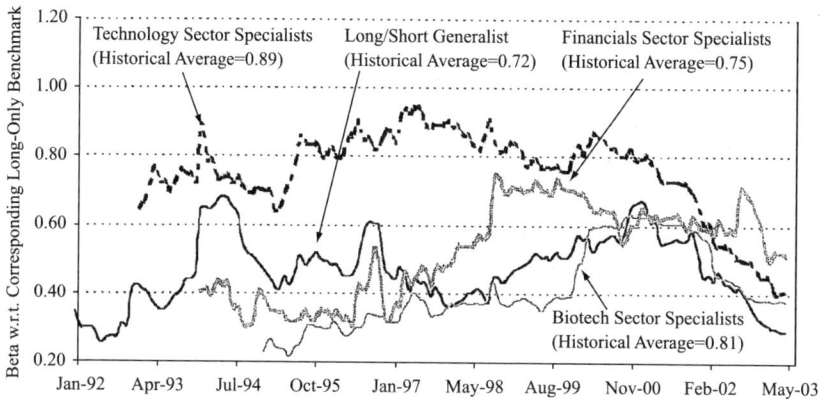

Exhibit 2   Two-Year Trailing Betas: Generalists Versus Sector Specialist

betas for the Long/short equity indices (both generalists and sector specialists) with respect to their corresponding long only benchmarks. The results are shown in Exhibit 2.

As can be seen from the exhibit, none of these generalists and sector specialist groups offers persistent lower exposure to its corresponding market than the other. Some sector specialists Long/short equity managers such as in technology and financials have relatively higher betas than the generalists for most periods while healthcare/biotech sector specialists have lower systematic beta exposure to their investment universe benchmarks than the generalists.

Correlation is another relative measure of a manager's ability to protect his or her portfolio from market changes. Exhibit 3 provides the calculated two-year trailing correlation of the generalist and sector specialist hedge fund indices with respect to their corresponding long only benchmarks.

For most periods, generalists seem to have a relatively higher

119

correlation to their benchmark (i. e., Russell 3 000 Index) than sector specialists. However, there is no definitive conclusion we can make as to which group of funds is consistently better over the entire period we analyzed.

3. Graham-Harvey Measure

The volatility of the different markets in which Long/short equity managers invest is quite different from each other. For example, exhibit 1 shows an annualized standard deviation for the healthcare and biotechnology index of over 44% compared to 8. 7% for the broad market index for the evaluation period. While we should note overall differences in volatility among the strategies as a first order of observation, for the purpose of this study, it would not be fair if we compared two groups of funds without controlling for benchmark volatility.

Graham and Harvey [1996, 1997] proposed the so called Graham-Harvey (GH) measure to compare a fund's investment performance with a benchmark return-adjusted for volatility. To compute the GH measure, we levered or un-levered the benchmark to have the exact same volatility as the fund for the evaluation period. [10] The GH measure is the difference between the fund return and the return on the volatility-matched benchmark. A positive GH value indicates that the investor is better off investing with the fund. A negative GH value indicates that the investor is better off holding the combination of levered or un-levered future positions of the benchmark and T-bills.

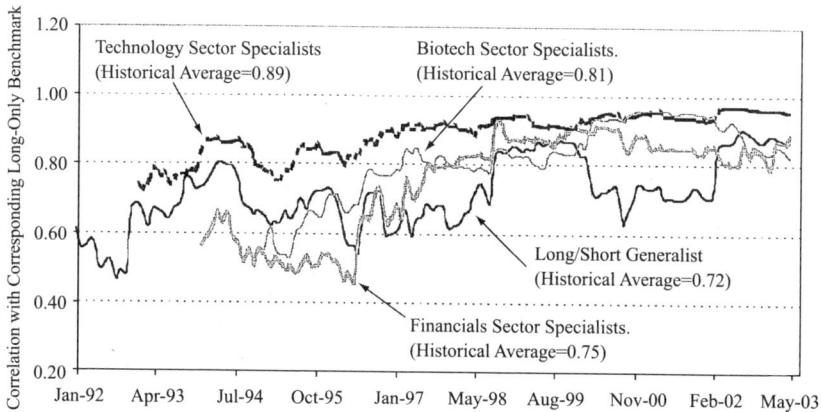

Exhibit 3   Two-Year Trailing Correlations: Generalists Versus Sector Specialist

This GH measure is very useful in this study because, as we discussed earlier, the comparison among generalists and sector specialists is meaningful only after adjusting for the volatility of each fund's underlying market in which they invest. In addition, the volatility-matching approach inherent in the GH measure is better because the performance of the funds is compared with the returns for a volatility-matched benchmark over the exact same sample period. Lastly, GH also measures the manager's ability to adjust his/her portfolio exposures as the market changes or a manager's ability in market timing. [11] This is certainly one of the most important aspects of portfolio management.

We computed the GH measure for each fund with its corresponding benchmark. Exhibit 4 summarizes the results.

Our results suggest that sector specialists have higher average and median GH measures than generalists. However, in terms of the percent of managers with a positive GH measure, there is no significant difference between generalists and sector specialists in our sample (87% vs. 89%).

Exhibit 4   Graham-Harvey Measure: Generalists Versus Sector Specialists

	Generalists	Sector Specialists
Number of Funds with Positive GH	207	90
Total Number of Funds in Sample	239	101
Percent of Funds with Positive GH	87%	89%
GH Measure–Average Value	0.68%	0.94%
GH Measure–Median Value	0.65%	0.85%

4. Manager Skill-Empirical Evidence

We measure manager skill using a one-factor Capital Asset Pricing Model (CAPM) alpha developed by Jensen [1968]. Alpha here represents the extra return that a manager earns over and above a portfolio with an average market or benchmark exposure. We calculate the t-statistics of the intercept of the one-factor CAPM model or Jensen's alpha. CAPM alpha or Jensen's alpha is computed as follows:

$$\text{CAPM Alpha: } (R_i - R_f) - \beta_k(R_{B_k} - R_f), \tag{1}$$

where R_i is the monthly return of the hedge fund i; R_f is the monthly return of the three-month T-bill; R_{B_k} is the monthly return of the corresponding long-only benchmark k; β_k is the slope or beta exposure of the fund with respect to the benchmark k.

Asness, Krail, and Liew [2001] and Liew [2003] use the lagged betas technique to adjust for stale month-end prices in hedge fund data. They found that hedge fund managers perform worse after adjusting for non-synchronous pricing issues. Similarly, we computed the summed CAPM alpha as follows:

Summed CAPM Alpha:

$$(R_i - R_f) - \beta_k^0(R_{B_k}^0 - R_f) - \beta_k^1(R_{B_k}^1 - R_f)$$
$$- \beta_k^2(R_{B_k}^2 - R_f) - \beta_k^3(R_{B_k}^3 - R_f), \tag{2}$$

where R_i is the monthly return of the hedge fund i; R_f is the monthly return of the three month T-bill; R'_{B_k} is the t-month lagged return of the corresponding long-only benchmark with k equal to 0 (no lagged), 1, 2, and 3; β'_{B_k} is the slope or beta exposure of the fund with respect to the benchmark k for t-month lagged with k equal to 0 (no lagged), 1, 2, and 3.

The calculation of the CAPM alpha or Jensen's alpha depends on the benchmark used. Again, because generalists and sector specialists invest in different universes, we employed different long-only market benchmarks for our alpha calculation to better measure manager skill. In other words, we tried to explore what percent of managers have investment skill (or statistically significant positive alpha) in the space they invest.

We define skilled managers as those with alpha (intercept) t-statistics of at least 2. [12]

After adjusting for beta exposures (again, with respect to each corresponding long-only benchmark) and for stale pricing issues, exhibit 5 shows that only about 41% of generalists and about 51% of sector specialists in the sample generated statistically significant positive alpha.

Exhibit 5　Historical Percent of Hedge Fund Managers with Skill:

Generalists Versus Sector Specialists

	CAPM Alpha	Summed Beta CAPM Alpha
Generalists		
Number of Funds with t-Statistics $>$ 2	101	98
Total Number of Funds in Sample	239	239
Percent in Skill	42%	41%
Average Alpha for All Funds with t-Statistics $>$ 2 (Monthly)	1.22%	1.19%
Average Alpha for All Funds in Sample (Monthly)	0.86%	0.84%
Median Alpha for All Funds with t-Statistics $>$ 2 (Monthly)	1.03%	1.00%
Median Alpha for All Funds in Sample (Monthly)	0.73%	0.72%
Sector Specialists-Combined		
Number of Funds with t-Statistics $>$ 2	52	51
Total Number of Funds in Sample	101	101
Percent in Skill	51%	50%
Average Alpha for All Funds with t-Statistics $>$ 2 (Monthly)	1.16%	1.56%
Average Alpha for All Funds in Sample (Monthly)	0.86%	0.96%
Median Alpha for All Funds with t-Statistics $>$ 2 (Monthly)	1.23%	1.23%
Median Alpha for All Funds in Sample (Monthly)	0.84%	0.76%

This difference of about 10% between the two groups of the managers seems marginal given the relatively small sample size of the sector specialists but we look forward to improvement in data collection and maturation of the hedge fund performance industry to see if there are indeed meaningful differences in skill between certain strategies and sub-strategies.

We also calculated the average and median monthly alpha for all funds in the generalist and specialist samples. As we can see from the exhibit 5, the average alpha with t-statistics greater than 2 for generalists was 37 basis points lower than for specialists while the median alpha of generalists was 23 basis points higher than the specialists. Specialists, at least in aggregate, cannot be dismissed as a fad resulting from the growth of the hedge fund industry; it would seem that preliminary evidence and indeed anecdotal evidence of many talented sector managers would support this.

5. Diversification Benefits and Manager Performance Under Various Degrees of Market Dislocation

The diversification benefit one receives from investing with hedge funds strategies such as Long /short equity is one of the most compelling reasons to invest. Many Long/short funds, especially those with relatively low net exposures, do not move as in synch with the stock markets as do long-only equity funds. This is particularly true in the context of declining investment opportunities in traditional asset classes. On the other hand, many authors (see e. g., Schneeweis and Spurgin [1998], Edwards and Caglayan [2001], Amenc et al. [2003], and Liew [2003]) have observed a dramatic increase in the correlations between hedge fund strategies and traditional asset classes when market conditions deteriorate significantly.

In this section, we investigate the performance behavior of Long/ short generalists versus sector specialists under various degrees of market dislocation. [13] We start with what we call the "first worst market condition" by selecting the six most negative benchmark months for the evaluation period. For example, for generalists, these occurred in

August 1998, September 2002, August 1990, November 2000, February 2001, and September 2001 when the Russell 3 000 Index had negative monthly returns of -15.44%, -10.64%, -9.79%, -9.34%, -9.25% and -8.93% respectively. The evaluation period is between January 1990 and May 2003. For technology sector specialists, these occurred in November 2000, February 2001, August 1998, September 2001, April 2000, and March 2001 when the Nasdaq Composite Index had negative monthly returns of -22.9%, -22.39%, -19.93%, -16.98%, -15.57% and -14.48% respectively. The evaluation period is between January 1991 and May 2003. Then we identify the "second worst market condition" by selecting the seven most negative benchmark months for the evaluation period, the "third worst market condition" by using the eight most negative benchmark months, and so forth. We continue this process until we have included all months in the evaluation period.

As mentioned earlier, we calculated beta exposures for the generalists and sector specialists with respect to corresponding long-only benchmarks. The results can be found in exhibit 6 where the leftmost point on the x-axis represents the most extreme market condition (six most negative months) and the rightmost point includes all months for the evaluation period. The beta estimates for each of the market conditions are depicted on the y-axis. As we move from the left to right on the x-axis, we add more data points in our beta calculations. Essentially, we move away from the worst market conditions toward a normal market condition.

As we can see from exhibit 6, the betas for all sector specialists are extremely high in the several worst market dislocations. The betas

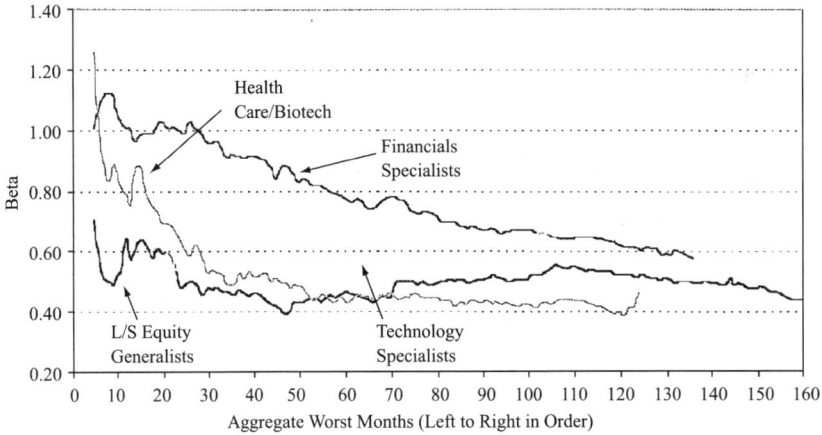

Exhibit 6   Betas Under Various Degrees of Market Dislocation:
Generalists Versus Sector Specialists

of the health care/biotech, financials, and technology sector specialists are 1.25, 1.00, and 0.87 in the first market condition respectively. Interestingly, the beta of the generalists in the worst market dislocations is significantly better than the specialists. For example, the betas in the first and second worst market dislocations for the generalists are 0.70 and 0.58 respectively. One potential explanation is that the generalists are able to diversify away the systematic exposure by moving their portfolio into certain sectors that may not highly correlate with the market (or Russell 3 000 Index in this study) during such extreme market conditions. Another potential explanation is that the generalists simply have better risk management skill that allows their portfolio to be less sensitive.

Next, we calculated the alphas for the generalists and sector specialists from the same data set, which are shown in exhibit 7. Clearly, all Long/short equity managers (on average) achieve positive (even higher) alphas when market dislocations occurred. However,

127

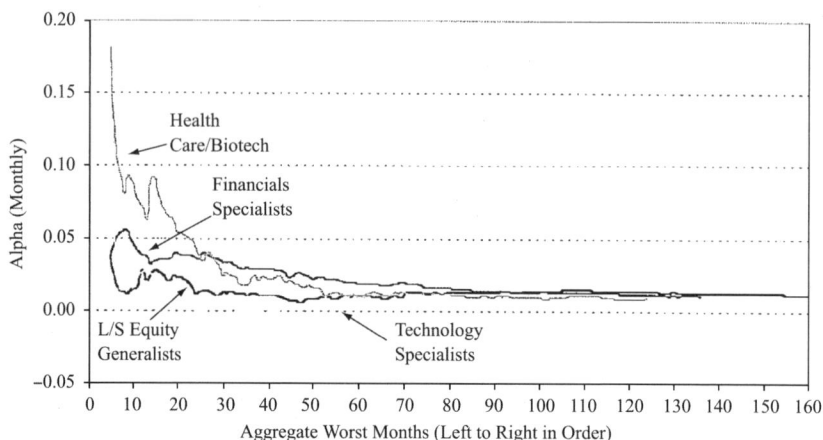

Exhibit 7   Monthly Alphas Under Various Degrees of Market Dislocation:
Generalists Versus Sector Specialists

there is no strong evidence to prove which groups of funds offer much
better alpha except for health care/biotech sector specialists, which
generated much higher alpha in the periods of market dislocation than
they did in normal market conditions. Thus it might make more sense
to gain healthcare/biotech sector exposure through a hedged portfolio
rather than a long-only manager.

Exhibit 8 provides the GH measures for all four Long/short
equity strategies. On average, all strategies have higher positive GH
values when market dislocations occurred. However, it is not quite
clear which strategy offers better returns after adjusting for the
volatility of the corresponding benchmark. The only exception again is
health care/biotech sector specialists who have much higher GH
measures in the periods of market dislocation than they do in normal
market conditions.

So far we have shown (in Exhibits 6, 7, and 8) relative measures
such as beta, alpha, and the GH measure for generalists and specialists

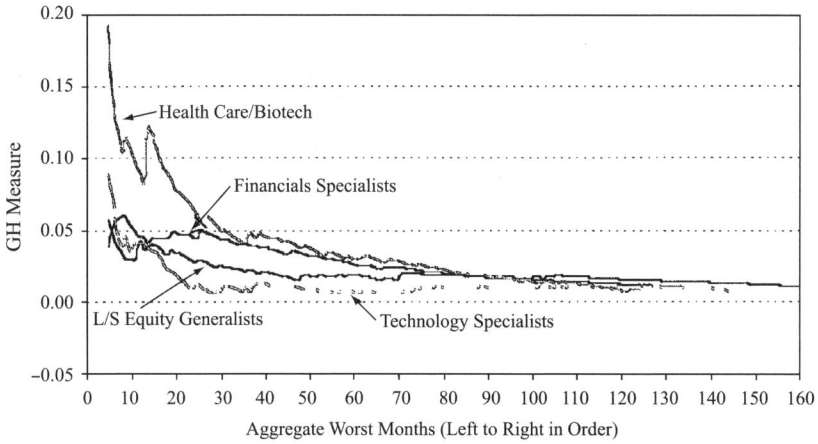

Exhibit 8   GH Measures Under Various Degrees of Market Dislocation:
Generalists Versus Sector Specialists

during various degrees of market dislocation. These measures are
calculated with respect to corresponding market benchmarks.

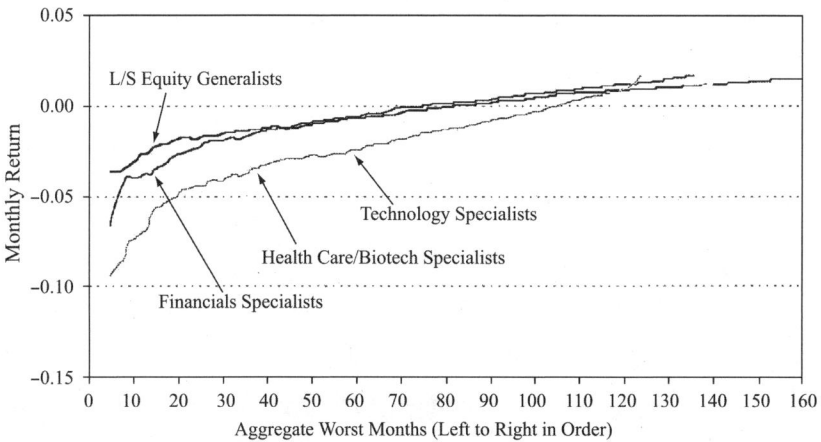

Exhibit 9   Monthly Returns Under Various Degrees of Market Dislocation:
Generalists Versus Sector Specialists

Exhibit 9 shows average monthly returns for all strategies during
various degrees of market dislocation. Note that these are absolute

returns, which are independent of any benchmarks or markets.

As we can see from exhibit 9, despite the superiority to their long only counterparts, all strategies discussed in our study have substantial negative returns in periods of market dislocation. This is partially due to the fact that most Long/short equity managers consistently maintain positive net exposure to their market. But the difference between generalists and specialists is significant. On average, generalists lost less than the sector specialists. For example, for the first worst market condition, the average monthly return for generalists is -3.68% while technology, health care/biotech, and financials sector specialists returned -10.76%, -9.46% and -6.66%, respectively.

6. Conclusions and Investment Implications

We have used various approaches to provide empirical evidence to compare Long/short equity generalists with three groups of sector specialists based on a sample of 340 Long/short equity generalists and specialists. Our study shows that there is no clear winner when investing in either generalists or sector specialists.

We have shown that the sector specialists as a whole are not better off than the generalists in terms of their exposure to systematic risks and their correlation to corresponding benchmarks. After adjusting for the volatility, the percent of funds with positive performance GH measures is almost identical for generalists and sector specialists. As a result, the market timing skill of both groups of funds appears to be roughly the same.

We presented evidence that skilled managers are not the

overwhelming majority within our sample of the Long/short hedge fund managers. After adjusting manager returns for benchmark exposure and non-synchronous pricing issues, only about 41% of generalists and about 51% of sector specialists in the sample generated statistically significant positive alpha. This difference of about 10% between the two groups of the managers seems marginal given the relatively small sample size of the sector specialists.

We also examined the diversification benefits and performance behavior of average hedge fund managers in periods of market dislocation. Our study suggests that the more extreme the dislocation, the lower the diversification benefits. On average, many sector specialists have higher correlation with the benchmark than generalists in extreme market dislocations. However, all strategies fail to provide adequate downside protection under the worst market conditions. Furthermore, after accounting for market activities (such as volatility) in a specified market, we have shown, using various performance measures, that there is no major significant difference between generalists and sector specialists when observed as a group.

While our study did not find evidence to support either generalists or sector specialists, this lack of evidence highlights to us the significance of choosing hedge fund managers largely through a "bottom up" process whereby individual hedge fund manager quality is paramount. Furthermore, the study did highlight some interesting differences between and similarities among generalists and sector funds that can be important when constructing a portfolio of hedge funds within a larger portfolio of multiple asset classes.

ENDNOTES

1. See TASS [2003].

2. As a comparison, event driven managers with next highest percent of hedge funds, manage about 17.33% of all hedge fund assets; see TASS [2003].

3. Different minimum time periods to qualify for inclusion in the study are largely a function of achieving a balance between a large enough sample (for example, sector specialists with a track record over five years are too few to be meaningful) and a comparable number of funds in generalists.

4. Strictly speaking, this index also includes some sector funds. However, we have found that the majority of the Long/short equity funds in the HFR database are generalists. Therefore, we believe that using the index as a proxy of the generalists will not have a significant impact on our results.

5. These are the three largest sectors in terms of number of funds. Due to an insufficient number of funds, we don't include other sectors such as Energy, Natural Resource, and Gold funds.

6. Our database comes from HFR and internal proprietary data sources.

7. The reason we use three (instead of five) years for the criteria of the sector specialists is to have a sufficiently large number of managers for the specialists sample.

8. For discussions on hedge fund survivorship bias, see, for example, Brown et al. [1999], Fung and Hsieh [2002], and Liang

[2000].

9. To some extent, we assume that both generalists and specialists have similar survivorship bias distributions or patterns.

10. Investors can always obtain such a volatility-matched benchmark portfolio by increasing or decreasing futures positions.

11. There is a direct link between the GH measure and market timing; for detailed discussion, see Graham and Harvey [1997].

12. T-statistic of about 2.0 (or 1.96 for more precise numbers) corresponds to statistical significance at the 95% confidence interval.

13. We use a similar technique to that used in Liew [2003].

REFERENCES

[1] Noel Amenc, Lionel Martellini, and Mathieu Vaissie, "Benefits and Risks of Alternative Investment Strategies". Working paper, EDHEC Risk and Asset Management Research Center, January 2003.

[2] Clifford Asness, Robert Krail, and John Liew, "Do Hedge Funds Hedge?" *The Journal of Portfolio Management*, Fall 2001, pp. 6-19.

[3] S. Brown, W. Goetzmann, and R. Ibbotson, "Offshore Hedge Funds: Survival & Performance". *Journal of Business* 72 (1999), pp. 91 - 117. Franklin R. Edwards and Mustafa O. Caglayan, " Hedge Fund and Commodity Fund Investments in Bull and Bear Markets". *The Journal of Portfolio Management*, Summer 2001, pp. 97-108.

[4] W. Fung, and D. Hsieh, "Performance Characteristics of Hedge Funds and Commodity Funds: Natural vs. Spurious Biases". *Journal of Financial and Quantitative Analysis* 35 (2002), pp. 291-307.

[5] John Graham, and Campbell Harvey, "Market Timing Ability and Volatility Implied Investment Newsletters". *Journal of Financial Economics* Vol. 42, No. 3 (1996), pp. 397-422.

[6] John Graham, and Campbell Harvey, "Grading the Performance of Market Timing Newsletters". *Financial Analysts Journal*, November/December 1997, pp. 54-66.

[7] Alexander Ineichen, "Asymmetric Returns". *UBS Warburg Global Equity*

Research Report, September 2002.

[8] Michael Jensen, "The Performance of Mutual Funds in the Period 1945 - 1964". *Journal of Finance*, 23 (1968), pp.389-416.

[9] Duen-Li Kao, "Battle for Alphas: Hedge Funds versus Long Only Portfolios". *Financial Analysts Journal*, March/April 2002, pp.16-36.

[10] B. Liang, "Hedge Funds: The Living and the Dead". *Journal of Financial and Quantitative Analysis* 35 (September 2000), pp.309-326.

[11] Jimmy Liew, "Hedge Fund Index Investing Reexamined". *The Journal of Portfolio Management*, Winter 2003, pp.113-123.

[12] Thomas Schneeweis, and Richard Spurgin, "Alternative Investments in the Institutional Portfolio". Working paper, CISDM, Isenberg School of Management, University of Massachusetts, 1998.

[13] TASS, "The TASS Asset Flow Reports". Second Quarter 2003.

Postscript

Long/short equity funds can be divided into two groups: Long/short sector specialists ("specialists") and Long/short generalists ("generalists"). Specialists are those Long/short equity managers who exploit opportunities and invest in only one relatively narrowly defined sector of the market such as financial services, health care, or technology. Generalists are Long/short managers who can invest across many or even all sectors of the market. Conventional wisdom is in favor of the specialists for their focus, dedication, and specialty on the sector. This paper explores whether this is true in terms of manager skill and diversification benefits. The draft was submitted to the *Journal of Wealth Management*.

Berens Capital was founded by Rod Berens in 2000. The years I spent there would go on to have a significant impact on my entire career and life.

On the one hand, Rod and his firm encouraged intellectual exploration and real research. I've written a lot of internal research notes, such as how to estimate extreme event risk; how to estimate hedge fund alpha from limited information, whether it's on the long side or the short side.

On the other hand, and perhaps more importantly, I have learned a great deal from Rod as to how to build up good sense and how to treat people. With his years of experience, he is objective and rational, giving him the ability to see through a lot of people and things. For example, whether Jack Welch, former CEO of GE, has contributed positively to GE's shareholder value; whether Jim Rogers, co-founder of Quantum Fund, is a real investor; how to evaluate the performance of Fidelity's famous star fund manager Peter Lynch. He very often offers his own unique objective and profound insights into the world.

In a sense, the specific tools and research methodologies were largely developed prior to joining Berens Capital, mainly at Dow Jones and Goldman Sachs, but it was at Berens Capital that I made a great deal of progress in building up good sense, which has had an irreplaceable impact on my professional life over next twenty years. I can say that without my experience at Berens Capital, I would not have been able to do what I have done for past 20 years.

My deepest gratitude to Rod.

I would like to dedicate this article to Rod Berens and other former colleagues at Berens Capital.

10

西蒙:活跃在科学前沿的博学家 *

　　翻开卷帙浩瀚的英美等国出版的各类百科全书(包括心理学、经济学、计算机科学技术等),总可以发现涉及西蒙(Herbert A. Simon)的条目,少则五六条,多至十多条,而这些条目又分属于不同的学科群,在社会科学和自然科学高度发展、专门化程度极高的今天,实属罕见。

　　西蒙 1936 年毕业于芝加哥大学,曾任卡内基工学院工业管理研究生院副院长(1937—1957 年)、卡内基-梅隆大学计算机科学及心理学教授(1966 年至今)等职。1943 年获芝加哥大学政治科学博士学位,并获得耶鲁大学等世界各地十多所大学的名誉博士学位。1958 年获美国心理学会杰出贡献奖,1975 年荣获计算机图灵奖,1978 年获诺贝尔经济学奖,1986 年获美国总统科学奖。他还是 20 个科学学会的会员。从西蒙的简历不难看出他渊博的知识背景,以及在当代极为活跃的边缘科学前沿的创造性贡献。正是出于这个原因,人们把他誉为当代最著名的博学家。本文对西蒙在几个学术领域的杰出活动做一评述。

---

* 定稿。发表于《科学》1989 年第 41 卷 1 期,第 66—68 页。

创建现代决策理论

　　决策理论(Decision Theory)是关于企业管理中决策行为研究的理论，是现代资本主义企业管理理论的重要组成部分。它认为，"管理的关键是决策"，决策贯穿管理的全过程。决策错了，生产效率越高就越没有好处。因此，企业管理必须采用一整套制定决策的新技术，以寻求最佳的方案。

　　决策理论分为传统决策理论和现代决策理论。传统决策理论的出发点是把进行决策时的个人或企业看成"理性的人"或"经济的人"。在决策时，他们的行为受"最优化"的行为准则支配，进行最优方案的选择——假定决策者的目标是固定不变的，有着全部可供选择的方案。这种理论是建立在纯粹的逻辑推理基础上的，是一种封闭式的决策模型。西蒙是现代决策理论的代表人物，他使用令人满意的行为准则代替传统决策理论的最优化准则。他提出，传统决策理论中的理性的人只有在所有措施和方案都是已知的，而且每一方案所能取得的成果也是可以确定的情况下，才能进行择优选择、做出决策。可是在现实生活中，决策者由于所处的环境和当时当地的条件，既不可能找到一切方案，也不可能比较一切方案，因此事实上不可能进行最优化准则的决策。最优化准则仅仅存在于逻辑推理之中，没有实践价值。

　　西蒙还研究了决策过程中冲突的解决方法，研究了管理行为程序化和非程序化的关系，以及创新的程序、时机、来源和群体处理方式等一系列有关决策程序的问题。全部决策过程从确定企业的目标开始，随后寻找为达到该项目标可供选择的各种方案，比较并评价这些方案，进行选择并做出决定；然后执行选定方案，进行检查和控制，以保证最后实现预定的目标。西蒙的决策理论是综合了行为科学、系统理论、运筹学和计算机科学等学科的内容而发展起来的一门边缘科学，它是从人类具有判断能力但又受到认识事物的局限这一实际出发概括出来的一套科学行为准则和工作程序。他把传统理论和行为科学有机地结合起来，既重视先进的理论、方法和手段的应用，又重视人的积极作用。诚如哥伦比亚大学商学院（Columbia Graduate School of Business）著名学者法利（J. Farley）教授曾经评述的："（西蒙的）最大贡献在于，他架起了经济学模型和客观实际世界之间的桥梁。"

1978 年 10 月，瑞典皇家科学院宣布，由于西蒙对"经济组织内的决策程序（Decision-making Process）进行了开创性的研究"，以及"西蒙的思想的大部分是现代企业经济学和管理研究的基础"，授予他 1978 年度诺贝尔经济学奖。

开创人工智能研究

1955 年夏天，在美国达特茅斯（Dartmouth），数十名思想活跃、有才华的青年科学家聚集一堂，围绕题为"机器能思考吗？"的讨论会开得生动活泼、气氛热烈。与会者有至今仍在人工智能领域起领导作用的西蒙、肖（J. C. Shaw）、纽厄尔（A. Newell）、麦卡锡（J. McCarthy）、明斯基（M. Minsky）及提出信息论的香农（C. Shannon）等人。会议第一次正式提出了"人工智能"（Artificial Intelligence）这个词，同时也宣告了这门新兴学科的诞生。

为了使机器能进行思考，就必须分析人的思维与推理并进行模拟。西蒙等人认为，人类思维的主要认识过程的模型是一个处理符号结构的系统，而不仅仅是数值数据的处理机；也就是说，人的思维过程可以简化成一系列的符号演算，可以被看成对问题求解的过程。这样，人工智能的核心问题就成为对非数值的符号问题的求解了。

早在 1956 年, 西蒙和纽厄尔就研究了所谓逻辑理论家 LT (Logic Theorist)的问题求解理论, 并将其写成程序在计算机上实现。其目的是希望找到人类在求解问题时的行为过程。他们试验了这个理论后发现, 它至少在一个方面是有缺陷的: 人们在求解一个问题时并不总是使用相同的控制过程(control process)(例如, 不同的数学家为证明相同的结论, 可能运用不同的定理和公理)。为此, 他们对理论进行了改进并编制了新的程序, 从而将人们在问题求解过程中已学到的控制过程结合起来。1957 年, 他们两人研制了世界上第一个用于人工智能研究的表处理语言 IPL(Information Processing Language)。西蒙将改进后的程序称为通用问题求解器(General Problem Solver, GPS), 将新的控制过程称为手段-目的分析(Means-Ends Analysis)。

这里所指的"问题"主要是一般性的问题, 而不是针对某一特定领域的问题。研究这些问题得到的结果可以推广到很多不同的应用领域, 也就是研究在解决各种不同问题的过程中存在着的共同的东西。例如, 如何应用知识进行推论和预测, 如何计划一个行动, 如何回答问题, 如何获得新的知识。

一个问题可以用一个状态空间表达出来, 其中的每一个状态就是一组事实的集合。求解问题的过程实际上就是从现有的状态转移到目的状态的过程, 也就是通过"分析"当前状态和"目的"状态的差别, 寻求某种"手段", 以最终到达目的状态。GPS 解决问题的方法可用以下 3 步描述:

(1) 估计当前状态与目的状态之间的差别;

(2) 寻找一个算子, 它能缩小第一步中所估计的差别;

(3) 检查在第二步中找到的算子是否能被用于当前状态。如能, 就用它来缩小差别, 并将通过这个算子达到的状态作为当前状态, 再回到第一步继续进行下去。

西蒙等人提出的手段-目的分析方法不仅至今仍是有用的人工智能技术，而且对科学方法论也是极大的贡献。近几十年的科学发展表明，人类解决问题的过程基本上是一种其过程为手段-目的分析的活动。其目的是：发现对通向目的状态的路径的过程的描述。一般范式是：给定一设计图，找出相应的"药方"或实现方法。很多科学活动是这一范式的应用：给定某自然现象的描述，找出能描述产生这些现象的过程的微分方程。

人工智能的研究为人类的学习、记忆和思维活动提供了新的研究方法和理论。1975 年，西蒙荣获了有"计算机诺贝尔奖"之称的图灵奖。图灵（A. Turing）是英国著名的数学家，他以首先设想人工智能计算机而闻名于世。西蒙获得此奖，是由于他把心理学、计算机科学和决策理论结合起来，开创了人工智能学科的研究，并取得了卓越成就。

认知心理学之父

认知心理学（Cognitive Psychology）是近 20 年来发展起来的新兴学科，主要是用信息加工的观点来研究人的认知过程和问题求解过程。

西蒙认为，"人的认知过程可以分几种水平：神经过程的水平以及初级信息加工水平（如从记忆中提取、筛选记忆中的字表，对简单的符号进行比较等）；或者是较高的心理过程（即问题的解决、概念的获得）"。认知心理学"不涉及神经过程"，那是生理心理学的事。它"主要研究较高的心理过程"，但也"并不忽视初级过程"，因为初级过程是高级过程的基础。认知心理学重视的是"初级过程与复杂过程的关系"。

西蒙和纽厄尔提出了"物理符号系统"（Physical Symbol System）

假设,这一系统把人类所具有的观念、概念、能力以及脑内加工的过程看成物理符号的事件,这样就可以把人的心理事件置于与物理事件同样的理论体系中来加以探讨。任何物理系统的事件、过程或操作,只要能用符号的形式表示,并能明确每时每刻的状态,就能用计算机模拟出来。同样,人类思维中的各种抽象概念和符号也可以像物理对象一样加以复制、转换、处理和相互连接。从此,符号和符号处理不再是不可捉摸的抽象的东西,而是可以客观描述和研究的具体过程了。

认知心理学使用的方法是通过分析人的思维过程,列出人的信息加工模型,交计算机模拟,以检验信息加工模型正确与否。传统的心理学研究方法无法揭示人的认知过程的本质。构造主义用内省法,通过受试人的口头报告来说明结果,实验往往缺乏客观性。行为主义采取直接观察的方法,比起构造主义来要客观得多,但是人的认知过程往往是无法观察到的。认知心理学要受试人在受试时,怎么想就怎么说,让思维像一匹脱缰的骏马那样自由驰骋;可以"说"得不连贯、不成句子、不系统,只要实事求是,想什么说什么。主试人通过对受试人这些"自言自语"素材的原始记录,分析受试人的思维过程,列出程序,交计算机模拟。如成功了,说明这个程序符合客观的思维过程,因而是真实的、正确的。这种方法排除了受试者个人的世界观、方法论、情绪等对实验的影响和干扰,把人的思维过程既是客观的又是主观的这一辩证关系有机地结合了起来,为研究人的深奥莫测的认知过程提供了工具,被认为是心理学在方法论上的突破。

西蒙在研究具体事件的计算机科学和研究抽象事件的心理学之间架起了一座桥梁,发展了不同学科之间的类比思想,促进了科学发现。如果不同学科之间的类比是合理的,那么,从一个已知的系统,就可以加深对一个不甚清楚的系统的理解。计算机和人脑,两者的物质结构大不一样,但是计算机程序所表现出的功能和人的认知过程却是类同的，即两者的工作原理是一致的，都是信息加工系统：输入信息进行编码，加以存贮，做出决策，输出结果。这样，就可以建立起人的认知模型：接受信息，编码和存入记忆，利用记忆材料做出决定，指导外部行为。同时，利用计算机作为实验工具，检验认知模型，看其是否正确模拟了人的认知活动。过去无法用实验来证实的人的内在的心理活动，特别是思维、问题求解等高级心理活动，现在都可以在计算机上得到证实，成为可以"捉摸"的东西了。而这些都是基于物理符号系统的假设，这个假说是认知心理学的理论基础，并正在经受理论和实践的检验，同时也扩展了计算机科学的研究范围。西蒙因此被公认为是认知心理学的创始人之一，他是世界上第一个获诺贝尔奖的心理学家。

西蒙不仅在上述的决策理论、人工智能和认知心理学方面有所建树，而且在政治科学、组织研究、公共管理、计量经济学、管理科学、运筹学以及科学哲学等诸多学科都有着相当深的学术造诣，出版了近 20 本专著，发表了五六百篇学术论文。

西蒙对中国文化也有着极大的兴趣，他取了一个中文名字"司马贺"。他是中国学术界的老朋友，担任美中学术交流委员会的主席。1972 年以来，他作为美国计算机科学代表团、美国心理学代表团的成员，应中国科学院的特邀，先后 5 次来我国访问。他多次与中国心理学界、计算机科学界、管理科学界的同行进行接触，交流学术思想，为促进中美友好和学术交流，以及人工智能、现代认知心理学在中国的发展起了重大的作用。

后记

1. 姚毓林. 消息传输协议 MTP 的 Petri 网模型和分析[J]. 微电子学和计算机. 1989, 6(1): 1-4 (Yulin Yao, Analysis and Petri Net Model of Message Transmission Protocol, *Microelectronics and Computer*, 1989, 6(1): 1-4, in Chinese).

本文主要为一个分布式系统的通讯协议提供了形式描述和分析。现在看来不免有稚嫩之气,但确为我发表的第一篇学术期刊论文。谨以此篇纪念孙振飞教授,没有他的鼓励和指导,就不可能有这第一篇论文!

2. Yulin Yao. Approach to Formal Specification and Analysis for Time Performance of the Concurrent Real Time System (RTEXS) [J]. *Elsevier Science Publishers B. V. Computers in Industry*, 1989, 12 (4): 347-354.

本文应用 Petri 网为一个实时并发的工业控制系统建立了形式模型并据此进行了分析。实时并发系统的分析在当时缺乏有效的数学手段及实现,德国科学家佩特里(C. A. Petri)提出的 Petri 网则弥补了这方面的空白。

这是我发表在国际学术期刊上的第一篇论文,投送时是初生牛犊,可谓不知天高地厚。国际邮费花掉了我当时半个月的工资,投送后有点后悔:因为将有好几个月没钱买书,对录用也不抱大的希望。

没有想到,半年后竟然收到录用函,仅需做少量的修改! 当时没有预料到,本文后来成为我成功申请佐治亚理工学院和哥伦比亚大学全额奖学金的基石!

本课题受到了青年基金会的支持。方明伦教授(时任上海工业大学分管科研的副校长)百忙之中为项目申请书写了推荐意见并参加了后来的项目鉴定会。

谨以此文献给方明伦教授——他在清华大学毕业后,60多年来为上海工业大学(后成为上海大学)工作,即使退休后仍然每天到学校,60年如一日,殚精竭虑,可敬可佩,是我终身学习的榜样。

3. 姚毓林. Petri 网:一种用于信息系统模拟的方法[J]. 自然杂志,1989,(12):883-954(Yulin Yao, Petri Net: An Approach to Information System Simulation, *Nature Magazine*, 1989, Vol. 12, No. 12, pp.883-889, in Chinese).

这是一篇综述文章,诚如《自然》杂志编后语(见同期第954页)所言:"Petri 网是 C. A. Petri 教授于 1962 年首先提出的。它是一种系统模拟的有力工具。60 年代末,国外有大量数学家、计算机科学家和其他领域的研究人员投入了这方面的研究。这门学科在国内远不及模糊数学那样为人知晓。本期发表的《Petri 网:一种用于信息系统模拟的方法》一文,通过实例,系统地阐明了 Petri 网的结构、图形表示和分析技术,以及其子类和扩充。可供读者领略这一领域的基本概貌。"

为了展开 Petri 网的研究,我多次到上海图书馆去查阅资料,短短的几个月复印了几百篇文献,复印费就超过当时我一个月的工资。为了节省时间,我自带干粮,一早等开门,待到闭馆才出。虽然条件没有现在好,但正是那段时间对研究的专注和投入,我才逐步形成了独立的研究能力,为一生打下了基础。

这使我想到了我的父亲。他十几岁进厂做学徒，后成为厂的领导，工作到六十几岁在同一个单位退休。父亲一辈子专注、勤奋和投入，不计较个人的得失，更专注于做正确的事情。他的大局观、对知识的渴望及对青少年时期的我持续鼓励，对我的人生产生了重大的影响。不幸的是，10年前父亲因一小事故患败血症去世，享年76岁。

我母亲虽然文化程度不高，但明事理、人缘好，含辛茹苦把我们3个小孩拉扯大。

谨以此文献给我的父亲、母亲、姐姐和妹妹。

4. 姚毓林，张逸敏，洪进. 基于Hopfield神经网络模型的启发式学习算法及其在数字模式处理中的应用[J]. 机器人，1990，12(4)：21-24（Yulin Yao, Yimin Zhang and Jing Hong, A Heuristic Learning Algorithm based on Hopfield Neural Networks Model and Used for Processing Digital Patterns, *Robotics*, Journal of Chinese Association of Automation, Vol. 12, No. 4, 1990, pp. 21-24, in Chinese）.

这篇论文是与洪进、张逸敏一起撰写的，使用Hopfield神经网络模型对有噪声数字模式进行识别，是国内使用神经网络进行图像处理的一个早期探索。

现在科技文献基本上可以网上获取，而那时候需要到上海图书馆检索，然后调出相应的学术刊物，再去复印。一般而言，每个环节都需要排队，我常常为了一篇论文的复印件，就花掉整整一天时间。

洪进是我在上海工业大学的同事，他在检测一室，我在二室。他参与了发型设计系统的开发应用，我们共事数年。他为人正直、坦诚、乐观和机智。洪进早我一个月赴美，先在康涅狄格大学（University of Connecticut）、后在纽约州立大学石溪分校（SUNY

Stony Brook）读研，我那时正好在纽约哥伦比亚大学计算机系攻博。我夫人烧得一手好菜，洪进经常周末坐长岛火车到曼哈顿来"蹭饭"，所以我们在美国也经常见面。不幸的是，他后来被查出肝癌晚期，每周一次在纪念斯隆-凯特琳癌症中心（Memorial Sloan Kettering Cancer Center）做化疗。那时我刚到高盛工作，每周二下午陪他回长岛的家。化疗结果有起伏。他后来闻悉上海一家海军医院有特别的医疗方法，所以决定回国就医。可惜，数月后传来噩耗，英年早逝！

可能洪进已有预感，所以把在美国的个人事务托付给我。即使在生命面临这样大的不确定性时，他仍保持乐观，令人印象深刻。

谨以此文献给洪进以及其他上海工业大学的老同事。

5. Yulin Yao. A Petri Net Model for Temporal Knowledge Representation and Reasoning [J]. *IEEE Transactions on Systems, Man, and Cybernetics*, 1994, 24 (9): 1374-82.

众所周知，知识表达是人工智能的一个核心基础，而时态知识的表达长期没有重大突破。本文用 Petri 网的方法，对最主要的 13 种（简化成 7 种）时态关系进行表达、分析与推理，以此来完善时态的知识表达。

这个工作最初是我在上海工业大学工作的时候开始的，然后一直到在哥伦比亚大学读书的时候才最后完成。我还记得在哥伦比亚大学上一门知识表达的课，由利特曼（Litman）教授来教这门课，她不要求日常作业，只要交一份学期论文（term paper）就可以了，我非常喜欢这种授课方式。记得我当时花了整整 3 个星期，完成了这篇论文。过了不久她就发来一封电邮，问能不能到她办公室去聊一聊。在确认是我独立完成后，她祝贺我解决了一个大问题，建议把论文送到 *IEEE Transactions* 上发表。正是因为有她的鼓励，我才斗胆把它递交给 *IEEE Transactions on Systems, Man and Cybernetics*。经过两次小的技术修改，论文于 1994 年 9 月发表。这也实现了我十几年前由吴立德教授触发的梦想。

我的本科 4 年时间是在复旦大学度过的。

复旦大学不仅有许多一流的教师（如吴立德教授），以及专业的指导员（如许德明和张世永老师），而且有众多才华横溢的同学。就以室友为例，本科前两年分专业前的 405 寝室，可以说是我们系最活跃的寝室，我 40 年后仍可以一下子叫出 6 位室友的名字：上铺赵文耘来自常熟，年龄最小，学有成就，后留校，现已成为复旦计算机系博导、教授；胖子罗从云，他的博学多才令人印象深刻；还有聪明的沈瑞华、顾海宏、朱玉霖以及北京来的马方。三四年级分专业以后，我的室友有：年少聪明的谢竞亚（上铺）、才华出众的胖子钱小民、张炳瑶、天津来的周斌、专注的庄青和林镛。还有跨寝室的周稚奇，我们是好朋友。按照当时老师的说法，我们这一级（8024）的努力程度，不能和 77 级、78 级相比，但我们许多同学出众的才能不仅体现在计算机领域，还体现在其他领域，如电影导演、经济学、哲学、语言学和数学等。我们的同学都做出了大量高质量的工作，令人印象深刻。

复旦大学的校训是"博学而笃志，切问而近思"，民间有种说法是"自由而无用的灵魂"。后者当时特别适合我：我 4 年里花了大量的时间在非专业上，无论是琳琅满目的讲座，还是丰富多彩的外系课程。

有趣的是，直到毕业若干年后我才发现，自己从内到外、从观念到视野，都早已被复旦大学"无用和有用的东西"充满，伴随着后来的人生之路。正是这些"无用"的知识丰富和造就了我的一生。

谨以本文献给复旦大学一流的教师、专业的指导员以及众多才华横溢的同学们。

6. Yulin Yao, Peter Allen. Computing Robust Viewpoints with

Multi-constraints Using Tree Annealing [C]. *Proceedings of IEEE International Conference on Systems, Man, and Cybernetics – Intelligent Systems for the 21st Century*. Oct 22–25, 1995. Vancouver. Vol. 2, pp. 993–998.

这篇论文是我在哥伦比亚大学读博时所做研究的一部分,主要关注计算机视觉里面的一个领域——传感器规划(sensor planning)。我的导师和师兄之前已开发了一个机器视觉规划系统(machine vision planner),其主要贡献在于为各个任务约束提供了一个显式的解决方案,并确定了一组传感器参数。但是,这个系统很难计算出同时满足所有特征约束的一个稳健或鲁棒性视点(robust viewpoints)。这篇论文主要将这个问题转化成一个无约束的非线性优化问题,然后应用树状退火技术(tree annealing)来计算解决这个问题。结果表明,即使在存在大量噪音的情况下,这个技术也能相当有效地获得稳健的视点。

我于1990年9月到美国,前面9个月在佐治亚理工学院学习。初到亚特兰大,语言不通,人地生疏,可谓两眼一苍茫。多亏有众多素不相识的同学的热心帮助:9月17日汪扬(哈佛大学博士毕业,当时已是数学系的助理教授)到哈兹菲尔德-杰克逊机场来接机的一幕,鲁明之(大气和海洋系的博士生)每周开车"shopping"及当学车教练的场景,每周与众多朋友踢足球及赛后大快朵颐的热闹,至今仍历历在目,仿佛就发生在昨天。汪扬现任香港科技大学的副校长,每当我聊到这些,他总淡然一笑,认为是举手之劳,而于我则是解了初到异国他乡的生存之危。

谨以此文献给我在哥伦比亚大学的导师艾伦(Allen)教授,是他提供给我在那里的学习和研究机会。唯一感到遗憾的是,我在哥伦比亚大学待的时间不长,许多工作没有进一步展开。

也以此文献给汪扬、鲁明之及其他佐治亚理工学院的朋友和同学们。

7. Yulin Yao, et al. Toward Parallel Financial Computation: Valuation of Mortgage-Backed Securities [C]. *Proceedings of IEEE International Conference: on Systems, Man, and Cybernetics – Intelligent Systems for the 21st Century*. Oct 22‑25, 1995. Vancouver. Vol. 2, pp. 1176-81.

抵押贷款证券(mortgage backed securities)的衍生物抵押担保债券(collateralized mortgage obligations, CMOs)是一种复杂且重要的金融衍生物，定价计算量巨大。20 世纪 90 年代初，一个 CMO 定价的计算需要几分钟或者几十分钟，这在瞬息万变的金融市场里是不可接受的。当时的华尔街公司通常使用大型计算机(如 IBM 370)甚至使用超级计算机(如 Cray)，但是效果不是特别理想。这促使我们对 MBS/CMO 的计算进行了探索，主要手段是把 CMO 的计算用分布式的方式进行并行计算，以达到快速运算的目的。

谨以此文献给道琼斯德励(Dow Jones Telerate)的琳达·贝克尔(Linda Becker)，是她把我这个金融零知识甚至不知抵押贷款(mortgage)为何物的外行带进了金融行业。还要感谢我的好朋友、好同事菲尔·恩妮(Phil Enny)，感谢琳达和菲尔。正是因为有了她们的支持和鼓励，才使得我能进入一个全新的行业，并在 30 多年后仍乐此不疲。

8. Yulin Yao. A Trinomial Dividend Valuation Model [J]. *Journal of Portfolio Management*. 1997, 23 (4): 99-104.

本文提出的"三项式红利估值模型"对金融学中最流行的证券估值模型之一进行了改进，并对 5 家公用事业公司的估值方案进行了检验。与"戈登模型"的早期形式相比，该模型显示出更好的结果。

由于道琼斯德励的琳达·贝克尔因故而长期休病假，我也决定离开。我加入了纽约高盛的全球市场风险管理及资产配置部。高盛在华尔街上一向以工作时间长、工作严谨及追求高质量而著名。

在高盛工作期间，我同时开始了在纽约大学斯特恩商学院"part-time MBA"的学习，历时 3.5 年。

回顾往事，这可能是人生最紧张的 3.5 年时间。除了高盛的日常工作以外，我一般晚上 8 点到 10 点在学校上课，每周工作学习至少 100 个小时，每天睡眠平均不超过 5 小时。

在这样紧张的环境下，兼职学习很容易被放弃或推迟。但斯特恩商学院的教授以他们对所在领域的深刻理解和对教学的热情，始终吸引我在那里如饥似渴地学习。教授们不仅以世界一流的研究著称，同时也有很强的教学热情，对学生关怀备至。当时马丁·格鲁伯已经是著名教授，对上他课的 MBA 学生还是花了相当多的时间。正是因为有他的鼓励，我才送交了这篇论文给 *Journal of Portfolio Management*。因学业成绩优秀，我被评为斯特恩学者（Stern Scholar），当时每年大约只有 1% 或 2% 的学生能得到这个称号，在"part-time MBA"学生中更是稀如星凤。

那是一段终生难忘的经历。

谨以此文献给以马丁·格鲁伯教授为代表的纽约大学斯特恩商学院的教授们。他们不仅仅是伟大的教师，也是各自领域世界领先的研究学者，吸引我这样一个外行，使我能够在短短的 3.5 年时间里学到大量金融和其他商业方面的知识，为日后的工作和学习打下了扎实的基础。

也以此文献给我在高盛工作的前同事鲍勃·利特曼（Bob Litterman）和杰弗瑞·威尔斯（Jeffrey Weiss）等，他们出众的才华以及勤奋和追求卓越的精神一直激励着我。

9. Yao, Clifford and Berens. Long/Short Equity Hedge Fund Investing: Are Sector Specialists Better Than Generalists?[J]. *Journal of Wealth Management*, 2004, Summer, pp. 35-43.

在多/空股票对冲基金的投资传统思维里，一般认为行业的专才基金(sector specialist)要比通才基金(generalist)更好，认为专才基金拥有对行业更深的理解，由此能产生更多的阿尔法(超额收益)。那么，到底是不是如此呢？本文在这方面做了一个探索，成文后递交给 *Journal of Wealth Management* 发表。

贝伦斯资本由罗德尼·贝伦斯于 2000 年创立。在那里工作的几年，对我的整个职业生涯及人生产生了重大的影响。

一方面，罗德尼本人及公司鼓励进行智力的(intellectual)探索和真正意义的研究。我因此写了不少研究札记(research notes)。例如，如何估计极端事件风险(extreme event risk)；如何从有限的信息来估计、推算对冲基金的超额收益，不管是做多的一方面，还是做空的一方面。

或许更重要的是，我在贝伦斯资本学习和培养了"good sense"(我一直找不到对"sense"最好的翻译是"靠谱"还是"见识"？)，这主要得自罗德尼的言传身教。通过多年的经验积累，他能够客观、理智地去看清、看透很多人和事。例如，如何看待那时甚至今天仍如雷贯耳的通用前 CEO 杰克·韦尔奇(Jack Welch)、与索罗斯共同创立量子基金的大名鼎鼎的吉姆·罗杰斯(Jim Rogers)和富达投资(Fidelity Investments)的著名明星基金经理彼得·林奇(Peter Lynch)等，他都有自己独到的、客观的、深刻的洞见。在他那里，我学到了很多。

从某种意义上讲，在我加入贝伦斯资本之前具体手段及研究方法已基本形成，但正是在贝伦斯资本的经历，使得我在获取"sense"方面有了很大的进步，对以后 20 多年工作的作用是不可估量的。可以说，没有贝伦斯资本的经历，很难想象有今天的我。

深深地感谢罗德尼！

谨以此文献给罗德尼·贝伦斯和其他前同事。

10. 姚毓林.西蒙:活跃在科学前沿的博学家[J]. 科学. 1989, 41（1）: 66-68（Yulin Yao, Herbert Simon – Active Learned Scholar in the Scientific Front, *Science*, 1989; 41（1）: 66-68, in Chinese）.

本文主要评述美国著名学者西蒙的学术生涯。对他的现代决策理论、人工智能和认知心理学的贡献做了介绍。

文章刊登在 1989 年 1 月《科学》杂志第 41 期上。《科学》杂志创刊于 1915 年,是中国最早的科学杂志之一。它的主要特色是对前沿领域的发展有宽广的视野。例如,同期发表的有时任中科院院长周光召教授的《中国科学和技术发展的历史、现状和展望》、西安交大汪英洛教授的《中国社会经济宏观模型体系》、陈省身教授的《在中国科学数学展望学术讨论会开幕式上的讲话》。很荣幸能够在这样一份历史悠久的杂志上发表文章,对我来说,其重要性并不亚于本书前面 9 篇专业论文。

* * * * *

在 1990 年出国前的短短 3 年多时间里,我主持完成了多个研究课题,在国内外学术期刊和国内国际专业学术会议上发表了近 10 篇学术论文,并主编了一本 260 多页的教材供本科高年级学生使用。

在编写这本文集的过程中,我有时也惊讶自己怎么可能有这样的精力和精神,在短短的 3 年多时间里完成了这么多的科研、教学工作,可以说是一个小小的奇迹。

有人说,世界上最强大的力量是爱情的力量,爱情的力量常常超乎我们的想象,它可以激发潜能,更能创造生命的奇迹。

陈英和我在 1987 年年初相识，此后的 3 年正是我人生最多产、最富有成效的时期之一！没有她的"激励"（"inspiration"），这一切就不可能发生！感谢我的岳父母培育了一个好女儿。

谨以此文献给我的夫人陈英以及两个孩子岱伟和岱菁，他们是我在过去几十年里前进的最重要的动力和源泉之一。

致谢

在本书出版之际,首先要感谢4位前辈罗德尼·贝伦斯、方明伦教授、马丁·格鲁伯教授和吴立德教授所作的精彩序言,它们给了我莫大的信心和鼓励,也为本书增色不少。

其次要感谢范景中先生向出版社所做的极力推荐,虽然因选题原因没有成功,但也因此得到一位业内资深人士在百忙中提出的许多宝贵意见和给予的大力帮助,其专业的精湛和考虑的周全令人印象深刻,对她的谢忱,深怀在心。也感谢陈先行先生所做的出版推荐。崔先生重新绘制了本书所有的图表,大大提高了它们的展示质量,谢谢他的敬业精神。

这本书得以在复旦大学出版社出版,离不开复旦大学林晖教授的大力推荐,也离不开资深编辑梁玲女士的欣然接受,她在教科书出版的繁忙季节,仍拨冗给予指导,本书的照片插页就来自她的建议。本书收录的10篇论文分别以中文和英文发表在国内外多种学术期刊上。这些期刊对论文发表的格式都有特定的要求,尤其是对数学符号和公式的处理几乎没有相同的。梁女士和她的同事细心阅读全部书稿,指出文中表达的多处错误,并统一了所有论文的数学符号和公式的表达,对他们的专业精神和一丝不苟的态度表示由衷的感谢。本书能在母校出版社出版,意义非凡。

在成书过程中,我的同事徐一粟、贾凡和赵心好利用周末的时间,或编排目录,或逐字逐句通读序言和后记部分,提出了不少建设性的修改意见。夫人陈医生通读全书多遍并关注到诸多细节，在此一并致谢！

感谢他们所有人在过去一年多时间里的帮助，使得本书能呈现在大家面前。当然，书中的任何错误和缺点由我承担责任。

父亲于 2014 年 11 月去世，谨以此书的出版纪念他逝世 10 周年。

2024 年 9 月

图书在版编目(CIP)数据

春华秋实 饮流怀源:我的计算机与金融研究:
1989—2004/姚毓林著. --上海:复旦大学出版社,
2025. 1 -- ISBN 978-7-309-17680-3

Ⅰ. F830. 49

中国国家版本馆 CIP 数据核字第 2024JX7360 号

春华秋实 饮流怀源:我的计算机与金融研究(1989—2004)
姚毓林 著
责任编辑/梁 玲

复旦大学出版社有限公司出版发行
上海市国权路 579 号 邮编:200433
网址:fupnet@ fudanpress. com http://www. fudanpress. com
门市零售:86-21-65102580 团体订购:86-21-65104505
出版部电话:86-21-65642845
江阴市机关印刷服务有限公司

开本 787 毫米×1092 毫米 1/16 印张 11.5 字数 144 千字
2025 年 1 月第 1 版
2025 年 1 月第 1 版第 1 次印刷

ISBN 978-7-309-17680-3/G · 2638
定价:99. 00 元